"Stephen and I have known Cathy and her family as their pastors since we first came to Hills Church in the Eastern suburbs of Melbourne back in 2005. Since then, we have forged not only a great ministry partnership but also a deep friendship. Having grown up in Africa myself, I have loved this connection that Cathy and I both share. From the outset, Cathy's ability to bring her African background to life is captivating but there is so much more to this story than the many countries she has called 'home'.

This story will take you on a journey through constant change, grief, loss, struggle, disappointment and tragedy, and yet, more than the tears of a broken hearted daughter and the prayers of a godly mother, is the faithfulness of an unseen but very present Heavenly Father who intricately writes His own story over the details of this disillusioned and broken hearted young woman, drawing her to faith in Him and inviting her to experience his grace and power to make something beautiful out of her story. The reader is left with an overwhelming sense that the same invitation is available to all of us."

STEVE and JENNY MAZEY
Senior Pastors, Hills Church, Melbourne, Australia
www.hillschurch.com.au

"The Rhode to Zimkesalia is a story of God's faithfulness. Cathy writes with a vulnerability about her life. She shares not only the mountain top experiences but the deep valleys that she has walked through. I encourage you as you read Cathy's story to have an open heart to the healing power that is available to each one of us when we walk in relationship with God."

        SAMANTHA JACKEL
        International Speaker and Author of *My Purple Pants*
        www.mypurplepants.com

"We all carry the burden of past mistakes but not many have the courage to share their story. Cathy has shared her journey of transformation through pain, tragedy and triumph. Hearing her story will make it easier for each of us to share our story. My interpretation of a Eugene Peterson quote is that Christianity is simply one beggar showing another beggar where to find bread, and Cathy is pointing us in the direction of the bread."

        DAVID MOLYNEUX
        Pastor, Warrandyte Community Church

A true story of restored hope and God's unwavering faithfulness

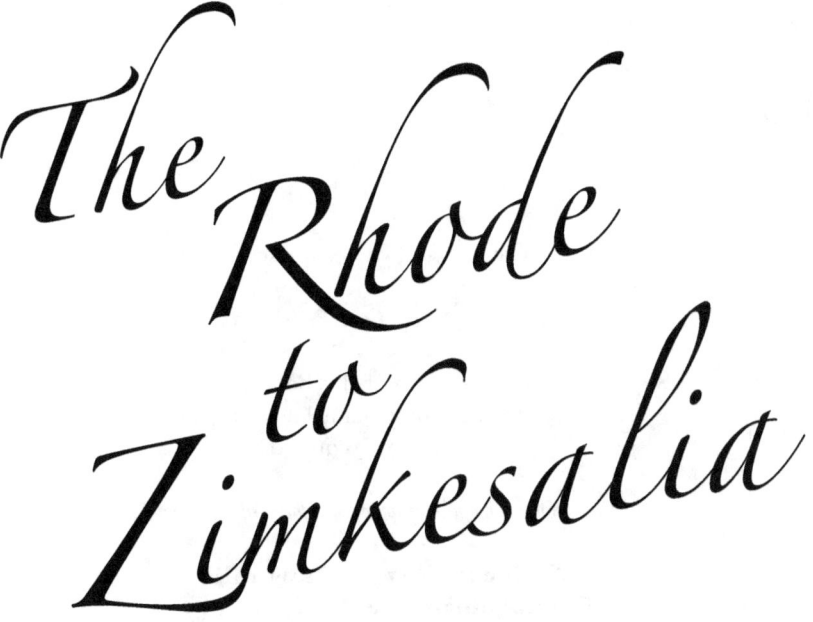

— Navigating through fear, failure and loss

CATHY SCOTT

Step Out Publications

© 2015, Cathy Scott, www.cathyscott.com.au

Published by **Step Out Publications**

Reproduction of elements of this book is allowable for non-commercial use only but acknowledgement of authorship is required.

Please Note: some names have been changed for privacy.

**National Library of Australia
Cataloguing-in-Publication entry:**
Creator: Scott, Cathy J. (Cathy Janet), 1965-author
Title: The Rhode to Zimkesalia:
a true story of restored hope and
God's unwavering faithfulness, navigating
through fear, failure & loss / Cathy Scott.
ISBN: 9780994387103 (paperback)
Dewey Number: 920.720994

All text, poems and photos by **Cathy Scott**
unless otherwise indicated.
Cover artwork by **Cathy Scott.**
Other illustrations by **Sarah Scott**:
www.facebook.com/StudioEsseAustralia
Cover and Book layout by: **Cameron Semmens**
www.webcameron.com

Dedication

I dedicate this book to my Mum, Bonnie Cormack – a woman who faithfully loved God and set an example of living her faith through trial and suffering. Mum, you will forever be my inspiration.

Contents

	Foreword	…8
	Introduction:	
	I hated writing essays, yet here I am	…10
	No more a survivor, now a thriver	…11
1…	An African backdrop	…17
2…	Fear sprinkled memories, moments and moves	…25
3…	Faith, flings and feelings	…35
4…	Cancer	…45
5…	Kenyan adventures	…51
6…	Turbulent times	…55
7…	New horizons	…65
8…	The man, David	…69
9…	Shock news, nausea and never a day to waste	…71
10…	Choices and commitment	…77
11…	Settling, sandpaper and seasons of serenity	…83
12…	Building our family	…87
13…	Our first family holiday	…101
14…	Overseas travels	…103
15…	Family expansion	…105
	PHOTO GALLERY	…108
16…	His dad, my mum and an imminent move	…127
17…	And we're off!... to resettle and adapt!	…131
18…	Trusting in the tough times	…137

19...	Anchored in the storm	...143
20...	Miscarriage	...147
21...	Jesse	...151
22...	Dad meets Rosa	...163
23...	My dear brother Jim	...167
24...	Hope rises with new life	...173
25...	Family reflections	...175
26...	Mom's visits	...181
27...	Keeping the faith – let's get practical	...183
28...	I don't fit in – where is home?	...195
29...	Therefore, do not lose heart	...199
30...	Rise up and overcome!	...209
31...	My commitment	...217
32...	Our Aussie life	...219
	Post Script: It's not over yet!	...208
	Thank you	...223
	Your Response	...224
	Bibliography	...226

*F*OREWORD

This is the true story of the awesomeness of a faithful God and the resilience, courage, fortitude and faith of Cathy's life journey. Her ability to rise up and trust God again and again, one painful and often tragic experience after the other, is encouraging and inspiring. The outpouring of favour and blessings that fulfill the promise that "our Father will never leave or forsake you" are always there. After reading this story you will have no doubt that no matter what you face in life, God is faithfully committed to seeing you through.

>   GLENDA WATSON-KAHLENBERG
>   *Pastor, Founder of Restoration Ministries*
>   *International. Author of 'Restoring Dignity'*
>   *and 'Restoring the Truth About Godly Intimacy'*
>   *www.restorationministries.co.za*

Through It All

*An overview of my journey so far:
a journey through the mountain top experiences
and the valleys
a journey just part way, a life not done
incomplete.
Revelations, which insert at places unknown
insights and lessons learned along the way
God moments and instances captured in memory
times of immense joy
and those of loss.
A journey not alone but with a Companion
whose rod and staff have comforted me
who never leaves
the One who has promised to walk the journey
alongside
whose Spirit continues to walk each day with me
The Great I Am
Faithful
True
A journey that at times I have wished away
at times I have wished to relive, to change
to do again
but always a sense of His presence, right there
alongside, inside
through it all.*

Introduction

I hated writing essays, yet here I am, writing a book!

It was Tuesday March 25, 2003 when I began to write this down. I have felt compelled to write some of my journey through life, trusting that my story will testify to God's goodness, mercy, grace and faithfulness. I pray that you, the reader, will find hope in what might be a hopeless situation and joy where perhaps it seems that joy can never be found again. We all have a story.

What you will read in my story is only a portion of my life. Bear in mind that it is my perspective of how things were and are. I have tried to keep details as accurate as I know them. However, they are my memories as I recall them. I acknowledge that people known to me may see things differently but this story is my perspective. You are about to read my experiences and intertwined through my story is the journey of my faith and belief in God.

I have been honest and open—in fact very vulnerable. I ask you, the reader, to read with the understanding that I have written as openly as I can as a means of being real, of not glossing over the messy bits, as a means of bringing healing to my own soul and hopefully, in some way, to you too.

I also feel it's important to mention that I do understand that not everyone has had the upbringing and worldview I have had. In saying that, I pray that if your views are vastly different to mine, you will not feel that yours are irrelevant, invalid or judged. I pray that in spite of our differences you will see the hand of God at work through my story and that He will speak to you in yours.

Things are always so much easier to understand in hindsight. I have gone through difficult situations and felt like my world was falling down around me but knew that God was holding the reins and directing me on.

I pray that as you read this account of my story, you too will experience hope and a life fulfilled in God.

No more a survivor, now a thriver!

The story of Joseph in Genesis 50 shows how his brothers intended to harm him but God was positioning Joseph to save his people from famine—God brought something good out of what the enemy intended for evil.

My journey hinges on a lesson learned and one I am still learning, that is to get a God perspective. God's perspective is truth; it is clear, uninhibited and untainted. When we look down on our lives from a heavenly perspective we get the bigger picture; we can see how those incidents and events tie in, how dark times bring balance and make the bright and colourful moments shine even brighter. It comes down to trust—if we trust Him with our lives we can know that He will make all things work out for our good.

Sadly, too often, we are deceived into thinking we are in control of our lives. This is a lie of the enemy.[1] We are not in control and are not meant to be. Independence from God is what caused sin to enter the world in the first place so we need to surrender, submit to God and allow Him full control. This leaves us free to trust Him. He will give us His perspective when we trust and we can relinquish the control we think we have and let Him live through us. He takes our broken pieces and makes something beautiful out of them—

1... The enemy: Satan. Adversary of God and His purposes.

if we trust.

Romans 8:28 (NLT) says *"And we know that God causes everything to work together for the good of those who love God and are called according to his purpose for them."*

In life there are seasons. It takes all four seasons to bring about fruitfulness, the harvest; all seasons make a whole, a fullness. In life, we tend to only want the easy seasons—spring and summer. We're less inclined to embrace the winters, the wilderness and barren times. The reality is we need all of them. In balance there lies a healthy life and much fruitfulness. God's desire is to allow all seasons to bring balance and He will enrich our lives through those seasons if we surrender and let Him.

I believe a key is to stay anchored; to be firmly grounded in Him, through whichever season we're in, holding fast to His truth. We may be tossed about and the storms will come but if we remain firmly connected to Jesus, we are sure to weather life's storms and seasons.

The reality is that sometimes life sucks. That's the way it just plain is sometimes. I know God is a Sovereign God but I also know He is real and open to us being able to bare our souls and allow Him to remove the destructive roots that entwine themselves around our spiritual organs, choking the life out of them. He is in control and He is the surgeon who must cut and scrape away the rot—the gardener who pulls out the weeds by the roots. Sometimes we're left with scars—reminders of what's happened to us but they need not inhibit us from living fully.

In John 10:10 (NLT) Jesus talks about the enemy—Satan saying *"The thief comes only to steal and kill and destroy; I have come that they may have life, and have it to the full."* We all have a choice to believe the TRUTH or to believe the LIE. When we choose to believe the lie instead of the truth, we let Satan rob us of years of our lives.

God's perspective is truth. The way I view God has influenced how I believe He comes through for me too. He is my rock, my strength, my shield, my hope. His Word is trustworthy. I choose to pay attention to what His Word says about me.

As I have been writing this book, I have uncovered layer upon layer of lies over my life, but God is graciously setting me free and I am now experiencing life in a much fuller way than ever. I feel as though I am more aware of how things have connected and impacted me. I feel awake instead of asleep. I am also certain that there are more layers to be dealt with as time goes on but, thankfully, He deals with one at a time and each layer brings more freedom and joy!

We can either survive or thrive. Sometimes, unfortunately, we can be misled, thinking we are thriving, when in fact we are merely surviving. When we become aware of what's really going on, we can decide to live a purpose-filled life of freedom the way God intended us to.

I awoke one morning with a mental picture that I believe God gave me which demonstrates this. This is the analogy I saw: We were formed in our mother's womb, a water encased balloon, where we could thrive because we were connected to a life source—our mother. As soon as we are born we become disconnected from that life source and must survive without that physical connection.

We often live our lives trying to be fish. Let me explain. We live in the natural world (the ocean) and when we need God because we are gasping for Him like the air we need to breathe, we come up, encounter Him momentarily and when we feel ok again, sink back into the ocean and forget about Him. God created us to breathe with lungs, not gills, with the Holy Spirit flowing through every part of us, not our natural, wilful ways. The ocean is like life in the world without God; the air is life with God: Kingdom living. God created us to live empowered by His Holy Spirit (our life source in the world) to thrive by His Spirit and not to just survive by our own finite means. As humans, we like the comforts of the flesh, the way we know how to do things—the way we think is better—our own way. We prefer to live underwater, trying to survive there, coming up occasionally for a desperate breath of oxygen to survive. Our searing lungs are burning for that life giving air (God) but we often wait until we're almost passing out before we surrender to our need for it.

To what life source will we choose to be connected? Are we trying to survive underwater when we were designed to thrive above it? Are we muddling through life ignoring God, trying to solve our problems without Him, desperately starving our very beings of His life giving Spirit?

Searing lungs, like our desperate situations, may cause us to come up gasping, longing for breakthrough. As we take a deep gulp of life giving oxygen, we might encounter God but then we go back down into the depths of the water, the daily grind of barely surviving, a place that we weren't meant to live, until the next time we surface, gasping again for what we need (Him). God designed us to live a life free of the encumbrances of the weight of the world.

My story is that of a survivor. However, I'm more than that. I'm now a thriver. I choose daily to live in freedom and I want to share my journey with you.

Psalm 23

The Lord is my shepherd;
I have all that I need.
He lets me rest in green meadows;
He leads me beside peaceful streams.
He renews my strength.
He guides me along right paths,
bringing honor to his name.
Even when I walk through the darkest valley,
I will not be afraid,
for you are close beside me.
Your rod and your staff
protect and comfort me.
You prepare a feast for me
in the presence of my enemies.
You honor me by anointing my head with oil.
My cup overflows with blessings.
Surely your goodness and unfailing love
will pursue me all the days of my life,
and I will live in the house of the Lord
forever.

New Living Translation

The Rhode to Zimkesalia

1
An African backdrop

Africa.

Words attempt inadequately to describe this diverse and amazing continent.

My home.

Hot and dusty, freezing and frosty, long grasses as far as the eye can see and beautiful plains dotted with wildlife.

Chequered fields of crops and grazing land interspersed with untouched rugged beauty.

Jacarandas and other stunningly beautiful trees of all shapes and sizes. Thorn bushes with thorns as thick and long as fingers—vicious!

Rare and wild flowers, all colours of the spectrum. Lush green forests and formidable jungles. Stained red earth, contrasting with white beaches strewn with seaweed and driftwood.

Large and small rocky outcrops, endless desert sands so dry. Ominous, enormous balancing rocks, rolling hills, majestic mountains, some sprinkled with the white dust of snow.

Raging rivers, waterfalls tumbling down like mighty beings alive and misty, wispy falls falling from on high and trickling streams and swamps.

White, fluffy rolling clouds, grey and almost black

clouds, accompany deafening thunderstorms, lightning and floods.

Such diverse and unique beauty. Scattered wildlife, as varied and numbered as the sands on the shore.

Hauntingly unique music and drum beats.

A scarcity and yet abundance of food—some bland and yet filling tummies, some deliciously different.

The rich and heady fragrances of life in Africa send you reeling in pure delight or revulsion. A passionate concoction of nationalities, languages, races, tribes and cultures. War, greed, crime, tension and tribal conflict—a normal way of life.

The people are deeply spiritual and of varying belief systems, differing faiths, paganism and witchcraft. Extreme standards of living range from overflowing wealth to utter poverty, resulting in a vast array of life expectancies—a fascinating assortment of culture and passion.

Africa. A sensual, inspiring continent.

A place where I was born and raised—a place indelibly imprinted into the fibre of my very being, so deeply implanted—a part of my DNA.

It was 1965 when the small landlocked country of Rhodesia, in Southern Africa, declared itself independent from British colonial rule. Civil unrest began building when the white minority government ruled a country vastly populated by the native non-white people. A grueling fifteen-year guerrilla bush war ensued. The warring parties were the Rhodesian army under the white government run by Prime Minister Ian Smith and the two main black tribal groups, who called themselves freedom fighters, trained by communists from Russia, North Korea and China.

Finally, the government was forced to hand over to President Robert Mugabe, of the Mashona tribe, who was a part of ZANLA (Zimbabwe African National Liberation Army)—the military wing of ZANU (Zimbabwe African National Union). The country then gained legal independence from British rule in 1980. Rhodesia became Zimbabwe.

Zimbabwe—a beautiful place so deeply engraved in my heart. I love the memory of my homeland where I grew up.

The town, Salisbury, now called Harare, was the capital. I was the first of three children born to Peter and Bonnie Cormack in May 1965. My siblings, Shirley (Shirl) and Jamie (Jim) followed.

Although the terrible, bloody war raged around us, for the most part as children, we were protected in the town. We regularly heard of people who had lost their lives. We'd listen to the communiqué on the radio often to hear the list of names of those killed and we lost a couple of our more distant relatives. We took precautions. Many people owned and learned how to use firearms but in actual fact, for me, life was okay. We were privileged that due to his pastoral role, my father didn't have to join the army to do his national service, unlike many of my uncles and friends' fathers and brothers.

The war became more obvious to us when we travelled to South Africa on holiday and would drive in convoy with military vehicles leading and bringing up the rear of the long line of holidaymakers heading for a safer place. I remember once we'd missed the convoy and decided to risk travelling alone. Of course, that was when Dad had to change a flat tyre and we lay in the ditch on the side of the road in the middle of nowhere, just trying to stay out of sight in case of ambush. It was scary, but kind of exciting too for a child who didn't understand the horrors of war.

There is much about the political situation that I purely gleaned from my upbringing and which, in some cases, I still have very little understanding of. Suffice to say that my impressions and information are gathered from my experiences there and yet in spite of being somewhat removed from the action of the war, I know it still impacted me.

Cathy Scott

My Reflections of Rhodesia—Zimbabwe

A childhood of innocence, crisscrossed by war.
Playing in the garden and climbing the trees
Aware of something that brought unease.
Having bags checked as we walked through the door
Trying to avoid another bomb at the local store.
Relatives, friends, going off to war
to fight for a cause they believed was worth dying for.
Schoolbags and belongings always held close,
with personal ID to prove they were ours.
Over and over we heard on the news,
stories of horror that made us recluse.
Ambushes, planes down, land mines and massacres,
people maimed in cruel acts of violence.
Sanctions, pressure, not understanding the fuss,
why the guerrillas hated us so much.
Misunderstanding complexities as a child,
loss was inevitable as the war was so wild.
It touched us all, the struggle for freedom,
there wasn't a soul who could live in abandon.
The innocence of childhood was marred by confusion,
The brainwashing, fear and struggle were usual.

Now as an adult I look back with deep sadness,
that life was so fickle at the hands of the madness.
Peace came for a while, things changed quite a bit,
But the hunger for power can drive many leaders
To acts of insanity, greed and profanity,
their justifications sounding pure to their ears
But really a build up of revenge through the years.
Now there is famine, loss of income too,
the land lies fallow, the people just stare,
Starvation, inflation, injustice and prison,
empty shop shelves, it's been turned into a hell.
A longing for peace still permeates the place,
it seems there is nothing, so little to save
But the people are gold, the land is rich,
if only it can again become the breadbasket from which
Wealth and food and love and peace
can be dealt to those who love the land and live each day,
trying to survive the onslaught of hate.
God bring sanity, peace and joy,
abundance and order to all the borders
Of the land of Zimbabwe, so fair and amazing,
The land of blue sky where the sun is blazing.

The Rhode to Zimkesalia

2

Fear-sprinkled memories, moments and moves

Growing up we moved—a lot! To this day, the longest I have lived in one place is about nine years. So moving has had a massive impact on my life. As I write, snippets of memories come to mind as I recall those different places and feelings. I share some of those here to set the stage for my story and to give you a brief picture of certain aspects of my younger years of life.

My parents were living in Triangle in the southern part of Rhodesia (Zimbabwe) and it was just a tiny country town so they travelled to Salisbury (Harare) when I was due and I was born at the Lady Chancellor Hospital on my mother's very first Mother's Day in May.

A little while later, we moved to another little town called Gutu. My memories of living in Gutu are few but remarkably memorable, considering I was so young.

I look back and can almost see myself in a little red jacket riding my tricycle at the side of the house. I hear a sound and, startled, I race up the driveway thinking my parents have gone out without me and I fall, grazing my hands and knees and, of course, I am very upset!

They hadn't left without me. I realise this soon enough when I am scooped up and comforted but I thought they had, as I'd heard a car drive past on the gravel road. Apparently I would talk about wearing my 'blumbar' jacket and falling off the trike onto the 'dement'!

At this early stage, I believe, the lie of fear and abandonment came into my life. A sense of mistrust, childhood imaginations and perhaps an awareness of the political climate of the time, the growing divide between whites and blacks, could account for some of that. I became fearful of getting lost and being kidnapped and a general feeling of being unsafe began to invade. If I voiced my concerns, I was just told not to be silly, that it was all okay but the fear was very real. I began to have two frightening recurring dreams which continued right up into adulthood. They were eventually cut off in Jesus' Name through prayer with the help of some praying friends. Only then did the dreams stop.

One dream was about a bus arriving at that house in Gutu, with armed African men shouting and running through the house and taking children away. I was always found under the bed, yanked out and made to get on the bus! I'd wake, trembling with fear and terror at the thought of being kidnapped!

The other dream was where I was being chased up a narrowing spiral staircase which wound itself up the side of a concrete grain silo—the stairs had no railing and became so tiny, I would be struggling to keep my balance, the pursuer would be closing in on me and then

I would wake just as I fell.

Just to make it clear, we had no television and I had not seen any violence or film footage of these incidents which could have affected me had I watched something like this.

On a happier note, the girl next door and I were friends and we'd swing on her tyre swing down the bottom of the garden and have so much fun! A shell of an old car lay abandoned in our back yard—a great place inspiring fun and imaginative play. I think she was my first good friend.

I have memories of eating guavas and especially loving the white fleshed ones—both pink and white guavas grew on the trees in the garden—so good! More pictures invade my mind of lush greenery and a garden tropical—on the edge of the bush, an oasis.

Colours of grey, blue and green striped the counterpanes on the beds in the room my mum used as a sewing room—the same beds I'd run and hide under in my dream. Random thoughts of a past life come to mind!

When I was about four or five we moved to Gwelo (Gweru) and I started school at Cecil John Rhodes Primary School. A feeling of unfamiliarity in the classroom and playground was horrible—I think from day one I was afraid. The whole atmosphere made me feel insecure and afraid and I don't remember feeling any love or care in the classroom at all.

As a Mum myself now, I've watched my children starting school and the environment seems entirely different. Today there is much more emphasis on making sure the kids feel comfortable, safe and happy!

It was also around this time that I became aware of my debilitating shyness. Whether it had its roots in fear or insecurity, it became a huge issue for me. It wasn't much of an issue at home but in public I began to feel that I would rather be invisible than noticed and wished I could disappear many times. Of course, this led to the start of my blushing.

People would comment and notice, often teasing me. That made things worse and I so often had feelings of utter embarrassment and shame that I could not manage to get through a conversation or situation. This ridiculous habit that I had absolutely no control over had the power to make me feel belittled and let down! Deep inside my heart, I knew I was able to do more, be more and express myself better than what showed. However I believe that at that young age the enemy saw an opportunity to belittle me by accentuating my flaws, my insecurities and shyness and robbing me of who I could be and was designed to become.

Our family pet was a golden Labrador called Shumba (meaning Lion) and one day his wagging tail knocked the tray of tea off the coffee table when we had guests. We also had hedgehogs as pets—what smelly creatures—thankfully their cage was in the carport. These are just a couple of random memories of that time that have remained in my mind.

One dark and rainy day as I looked out of the window and amongst the rose garden I could see a tall man with a hooded raincoat on. Not able to see who he was under the raincoat, I was suddenly afraid of this stranger so I ran down the hallway and hid under the bed in fear. As it turns out it was my Dad who'd gone outside to pick some flowers for my Mum—they shared quite a laugh that I'd been so afraid but I didn't see the joke. All I felt was immense relief that it was Dad and not someone threatening who'd materialize in my dreams.

I also have a rather amusing memory of being given a ring encased in cotton wool inside a little matchbox by a boy at school—his name was Simon. I was so excited and couldn't wait to show my Mum who freaked out and told me the ring was a real diamond engagement ring! She put me in the car, took me to this boy's house and made me return it! He of course, was in a lot of trouble with his mother who realised she couldn't leave her rings lying around again! I was quite indignant that they didn't take our 'engagement' seriously and of course, I thought it was very sweet of him – we were both aged 5!

I am sure all kids dream and wish they could fly. Well I was no different and there was a day when I was wishing I could fly so much that I made cardboard wings and got my Mum to attach some elastic bands on the upper arm and wrist so they stayed on my arms. I am certain she would never have put them on had she realised I would actually try to fly and jump off the veranda roof arms flapping wildly! It's funny now but wasn't then—with a few bruises and grazes as a result of my adventure!

One thing my parents did throughout our lives was invite people to stay in our home. Their hospitality extended to all. One of those people was a young teacher who stayed with us a few times over a couple of years. All I remember was how much fun she was. She played with us and made us laugh and she loved us. I recall looking forward to her visits when we were told that 'Aunty' Shirley was coming again.

I have come to realise the effect some of the more negative incidents had in my life—like thinking I'd been left behind, starting school, shyness and the 'stranger' in the garden. It's almost like a grey filter was placed over me through which I began to view my whole life and I became so accustomed to the hazy view, I didn't even know I couldn't see clearly. I believe these incidents were the beginning of a sense of insecurity, fear, abandonment and rejection which began to take a hold on me. There were more of these situations to come.

In early 1973, we moved to Johannesburg, South Africa, while Dad went to Bible College for three years. We moved around a few suburbs until we settled in Orange Grove and I attended Norwood Primary School. I made a few friends but I did struggle as all the kids had learnt Afrikaans as a second language from their first year in school (for many kids it was their first language) and I was coming into the system in the third year and didn't know a word of it! I had to learn fast but always felt a bit out of it and struggled to keep up with everyone else.

I remember walking to school most days, a couple of kilometers, and some days we got a lift with a neighbour. I didn't like living there—walking to school was another opportunity for fear to raise its ugly head and I became suspicious of anyone I passed or who walked nearby. I remember sprinting through certain sections of the route home and trying to get out of there as fast as I could. This possibly stemmed from the fact that I had lived in a small town in Zimbabwe and moving to a large city with many more people around, huge roads, freeways and traffic jams was quite overwhelming!

My sister Shirley started school at Norwood and one of my memories is of Mum having a little concern and a giggle that even on a hot day, if she came to pick us up, Shirl would still have her school cardigan on and be sitting there red-faced in the heat! I don't think she was very bothered by the heat at all! So cute! From a very young age, Shirley would 'teach' her dolls and teddies and anyone littler than her. Her desire to be a schoolteacher was realised once she grew up.

Our brother Jamie was a cute little toddler at this stage and, from what I can remember, a busy little boy who was full of life and energy! He loved to play with any kind of sports equipment, his favourite being a ball!

Other memories of life during this time in Johannesburg were of God's provision for our family. I remember the doorbell ringing a few times and we'd answer it and there would be a box of groceries anonymously given to us or an envelope with some cash. At this time, while Dad was in Bible College, there was no income. I began to see how God answered my parents' prayers and to experience His faithfulness. I recall the hilarious laughter as we'd dig through boxes of donated clothing for families of Bible College students trying to find something for each of us to wear.

I recall the wooden floors with some creaky boards and how I learned to find the boards that didn't creak under the strip of carpet in the hallway, especially if I wanted to sneak into the kitchen and 'steal' a Marie biscuit out of the sideboard cupboard! Of course I got caught a few times but got away with it a few more, and felt quite accomplished in knowing which boards not to step on!

Our family made good friends with a Christian family who lived near the school and who went to the same church as we did. They had a daughter who became one of my good friends at that time. We both played the piano and it was great to have that in common as well as both being avid readers.

I remember quite clearly the sense of loss I felt when news came of my Grandfather's sudden death from encephalitis. This was the first time I had lost a close relative and my father's grief and shock is something I remember clearly. It was also the first time I remember such pain. Dad seemed broken hearted and yet he was strong in his faith and always pointed us to reach out to God in our grief and pain.

I realise God's protection covered us kids as one evening when my parents went out (as I recall they took Jamie with them) they organised a man who was also a student from the Bible college to be our babysitter for the evening.

After we had gone to bed, he came into the room and tried to touch me inappropriately, causing me to immediately make the excuse of needing to go to the toilet, so I quickly took my sister into the bathroom locked the door and spent the rest of the evening in there.

In fear we sat on the floor next to the bath with towels around us to keep us warm and I recall a very strong protective instinct in me that arose as I tried to keep Shirley calm without making her fearful. My thoughts raced as I tried to figure out how we could escape out of the only tiny window that opened, high up in the wall above another window pane.

It was a long way down on the outside and it was so dark. So what would we do if we got out? What if he found us again? Where would we go? A neighbour? And what if Shirley fell on her head? How could I help her up on this side and then catch her on the other side? How could I get us down without making noise or breaking the window or hurting ourselves? Oh so many wild thoughts raced around like a whirlwind.

I have no idea how long it was that we stayed in there. When he called, wondering when we'd come out again, I used every excuse I could think of to stay inside behind the locked door. It took all my control to sound normal and not let my racing breath cause my voice to sound panicked. Thankfully, he never pursued us further.

A while later I heard my parents return, muffled voices and he left. It was only then that we unlocked the door and I told them what I had feared and how uncomfortable I'd felt. Oh my Mum and Dad held us close and comforted us—such a feeling of safety. I'd never been so relieved to see them!

Of course, my father was furious—I think I recall that this young man was expelled from the college as a result! I would have been somewhere between seven and nine years old and Shirley was three and a half years younger. I guess, in the innocence of youth, we hadn't realised the real danger we were in and I am thankful God kept us safe. Needless to say, my parents showed their love and protection by never leaving us with a man to look after us again!

The Tapestry Poem

Unknown origin, popularised by Corrie ten Boom

My life is but a weaving Between my God and me.
I cannot choose the colours He weaveth steadily.

Oft' times He weaveth sorrow; And I in foolish pride
Forget He sees the upper And I the underside.

Not 'til the loom is silent And the shuttles cease to fly
Will God unroll the canvas And reveal the reason why.

The dark threads are as needful In the weaver's skillful hand
As the threads of gold and silver In the pattern He has planned

He knows, He loves, He cares; Nothing this truth can dim.
He gives the very best to those Who leave the choice to Him.

3
Faith, flings and feelings

After three years, Dad graduated. He was called to a church in Harare and we moved back to Zimbabwe where Dad became the Pastor of a Baptist Church.

This was again a very disruptive time for us all and I became even more shy and reclusive. It seemed easier to withdraw than make friends. I compared myself to everyone I met—they were cleverer, had prettier hair, didn't have freckles like me, were more confident, more popular, had more friends and had lived there for a long time, so were settled. I was a late developer compared to my friends. They were wearing bras and starting their periods way earlier than I was and it merely reinforced that feeling of being different, never measuring up and being left out.

I had a teacher who went out of his way to make my life awful by making me blush all the time. I would withdraw and just wait for home time every day, wishing it would come sooner so I could escape the taunts. I remember trying so hard to be brave and actually being told that I was very brave when I was one of the only girls on a conservation camp, (where we dissected a goat) who blew up the lungs, putting the wind pipe to my mouth! Eeuw! The thought of it now!

It was during those primary years that I began to feel embarrassed about my father's profession—I avoided telling people that he was a pastor; I'd rather say he did anything else and would change the subject if I could.

However in contrast, I became more serious about my own relationship with God and began to share my faith with friends if they didn't actually mock me for it first.

While Dad was pastoring, I remember we had someone come to the church and talk about prayer, that it was a conversation with God and didn't necessarily need to be a long, fancily worded speech. A sentence could be a prayer—it should come from the heart, just like when we talk to someone else that we love.

I began to go with both or either of my parents to the early morning prayer meetings where we could 'practice' praying like this. I found my confidence to pray in public began to grow and discovered the truth and reality of a personal relationship with God. This was the one time I felt safe in public speaking—I could pray out loud and was not criticized but encouraged for it.

One day whilst walking home from school, I led a girl to the Lord and we sat on the side of the road as I led her in the sinner's prayer. I have never forgotten that day as I raced home afterwards and told my parents and they gave me a New Testament to give her. I raced back and shyly handed it to her. She was shy too but also very eager to read it. We talked often of the things of God after that as we'd walk to and from school, until we moved away—again.

During the time Dad was pastoring this church, my

memories are mixed. Due to the fact that we were living in the church Manse, Dad worked from home and was often in the office preparing sermons, praying or reading and such. I remember we all had to be quiet because of Dad's work and I think that was the start of some of my resentment which began to build towards the work Dad was doing with the church.

Understandably, I now know it wasn't the easiest job for him and he was doing his best. But he wasn't fun any more; he was always busy, serious and stressed out. To me, it was the burden of the church and church issues that began to take a toll and I remember sitting on the kitchen bench in tears one day telling Mum I wished he'd leave the church and we could go somewhere else! I also remember Mum agreeing with me that it wasn't an easy time but we had to trust that God had our lives in His hands. I don't think I was too sure myself that God knew what He was doing back then. I remember wishing my Dad just had a regular job like other dads and that we could be 'normal' – whatever normal is!

Another memory is of God's provision when, one day, a truck arrived at the house with a delivery for our family. This at first baffled my parents. The delivery was for them but they hadn't ordered it. It was furniture—as I recall—a lounge suite, coffee table and a lamp. I also remember a dining room suite and two single bedroom suites arriving around about the same time. I don't think they were a part of that delivery but a good second hand donation from someone or a purchase my parents made.

This was so exciting as the only lounge suite we'd had was a very old, burgundy/purple-brown and an extremely lumpy suite, not at all comfortable. As a girl in her early teens, it was very embarrassing for me to bring any friend to my house as we had such old and ugly mismatched furniture! This new one was very trendy for the day— retro now! I remember it being a mixture of mustard orange colours—vinyl chairs with small checked cushions! I was so happy our house wasn't so embarrassing anymore.

It is interesting how the ways of the world can impact a young person. My desire to be accepted and to fit in was so influenced by the accepted 'norm' of the environment I was in that it even extended to the aesthetics of our home. Perhaps that is one reason that to this day, I love design and décor and making things look lovely!

Early 1978 brought a time of excitement—Dad had a visitor. Through a series of conversations, he was offered a position at World Vision, an international humanitarian organization. They were looking for someone who had experience in five areas and Dad had all five. It seemed an answer to prayer and it wasn't long before we moved house to another suburb of Harare and Dad began his new job. I just remember the sense of relief I felt that it was a new start, a good time for us all. There seemed to be a sense of positive anticipation in my parents' mood.

What followed were probably some of the most stable and more happy years of my teens, living in Highlands, Harare, and attending a Baptist Church not far from there, becoming involved in a Youth Group and going to Roosevelt Girls High School.

I was certainly impacted by what people thought. I liked that our house was in a nice suburb; the house was decent (still not as nice as some of my friend's houses but way nicer than any we'd had before).

Church wasn't something I dreaded anymore. It was fun and I think it helped that I'd made some firm friends, some of whom I still have to this day. Youth Group was something I looked forward to every Friday night. It was a safe place where we could be ourselves in a fun environment and discuss issues of God and life on a level that was relevant to our age group. I'd often invite friends to join us and they'd stay over at our place afterwards. Socially, I was beginning to feel that I had friends and was accepted and I had a place where I fitted in.

Since the start of primary school, I had been sent to piano lessons. Some of the time I enjoyed it but, to be honest, most of the time I really didn't. Music, which seemed to come naturally to me (especially the syncopated style and jazz), some of which I could play by ear, was contrary to the music I was being taught. It was a classical style that became something I detested more as time went on.

At about the age of fourteen I started to teach myself to play the guitar. Now this was fun as I could play the songs I wanted to play, get creative, sing along and I could easily take it with me to play with my friends who had guitars too. I gave up piano lessons in my mid-teens and felt such relief! It had become such an issue of dreaded discipline for me that all the enjoyment and creativity had long disappeared. It took years for me to enjoy playing the piano again.

There are some that believe that, to learn something well, you need to be disciplined and stick to it even if you hate it—that it's good for you in the long run. To the contrary I believe that, if it becomes a military exercise and if creativity and enjoyment is removed, so is the passion and desire to persist even when it's not easy. The art becomes a dreaded chore, not a joy to enjoy the challenge of succeeding in.

Of course, there will be days of drudgery during the course of any type of disciplined learning but to have the fun of learning so squashed out of you that you hate it defeats the purpose—and that's how I felt about my piano playing.

Passions and creativity need to be encouraged and, sometimes, it's not the activity that is the problem but the method of learning, the environment, the attitude with which it's approached. I still recall the sting of the ruler on my knuckles as my teacher slapped my hands repeatedly if I got wrong notes and if I happened to glance down at my hands instead of keeping my eyes on the music notes on the page—usually by then I'd lost my way and was playing by ear anyway. I never was good at sight reading! I truly hated that woman and had to deal with learning to forgive her years later.

It was during my primary school years that I became an avid reader. Anything by Enid Blyton—the Famous Five, Secret Seven and Nancy Drew—were my favourites and then I branched out into different novels as the years progressed. The Narnia books, autobiographies, adventure novels, spy and mysteries, anything to do with the Soviet Union and books about Africa all intrigued me.

My reading became one of my places of solace; I could escape into another world and I loved it! One of my favourite things was to curl up with my book either on my bed or in an armchair and disappear into the pages of the world I was reading about. Thankfully, this was one past-time I was encouraged in. I was given the label of 'bookworm'.

It was also around my early to mid-teens that I began to notice boys! Of course, this was quite normal for my age and I had the usual few teenage crushes and flings.

However, my insecurities and desire to be accepted and loved made me feel that without a boyfriend I lacked worth. I went through a series of crushes and short teen flings, each one making me feel worthy and accepted while it lasted but quite the opposite when it broke off. In the back of my mind was an unspoken fear of never being worthy enough for someone to want to love and marry one day.

I had also made some firm friends and so it was with great pain in my heart when our family left Zimbabwe to move to Kenya because of Dad's work. I felt like my little world had been torn away. I hated that, at the age of sixteen, I didn't have a choice. I had to do what my parents wanted, go where they went against my will and I began to feel unheard. My complaints were ignored and I was told to make the best of it and that I could go back to Zimbabwe one day, when I was old enough to make my own choices.

It felt to me that, because of my age, nothing I said was actually relevant. I was too immature to voice any opinion that held any weight. I was expected to make the most of this experience, look forward to it and enjoy the challenges that would come my way. I felt that, because I was sixteen, eyes were figuratively rolled whenever I held an opinion differing to the adults around me.

To some extent, of course, there is truth in that. I was only sixteen, immature and had a lot to learn. However, all I could see and feel was more change, more discomfort, more being the 'new' kid, more of not fitting in and more of not belonging. I didn't feel heard. My heart would ache for familiarity and security; all I wanted to do was stay where I felt happy and safe. And I was torn as my whole familiar world was ripped away from me.

I was mostly thankful for my home life, since I really disliked school—being shy; changing schools so many times was difficult and making new friends quite painful. Home was the only place I could retreat and be myself. I recall deciding one day that I would just be a loner as it was easier to make no friends than to make them and have to leave again.

Home and my immediate family were the only constants in my life. Now that I think about it, being more comfortable at home is probably quite normal and most people would have some sense of that feeling I'd imagine. As I mentioned, my books became my continued escape and haven!

As I have grown older, I have seen how the enemy used my shyness to stop me mingling with people as I could have, to stop me being confident and becoming who God wanted me to be. I have learnt to navigate the journey through friendships much more easily with time. I realise that being different isn't all that bad, that sometimes it's a good thing and it's okay to embrace my individuality.

I also see how valuable it is to embrace other people's differences and diversity with acceptance and that God makes us all unique. With a little more wisdom, I have come to realise how important relationships with friends and family are and that, although not easy and sometimes torn apart, they are worth the effort in spite of pain and separation.

The reality is that to love is to risk being hurt. To gain the precious joy and value of friendship requires us to put ourselves out there, to be willing to accept the good with the bad. If we choose not to, we risk becoming isolated, lonely and depressed. Sometimes we only tentatively half put ourselves out there, out of fear, and we only experience shallow friendships but these are the ones that don't really satisfy. Of course we need wisdom here, we can't be close to everyone and we must choose carefully to whom we open ourselves up. But to never do that at all, is to miss out.

Not only do we miss out but also others miss out on us—on what we have to give and contribute from our side of the friendship. We are fallible beings. At the end of the day, people are just people—we all make mistakes. Forgiveness needs to be a huge part of our daily routine and relationships and the only One who never leaves or lets us down is our Heavenly Dad—our friend and father God. This is my experience.

The Rhode to Zimkesalia

4

Cancer

Growing up, we always knew Mum had some health issues. She had to be careful about her diet and couldn't eat certain foods. She needed to rest fairly often —her forty winks as she called it. She was one who never complained and so we really were unaware of how ill she had been in her life. Since childhood, she'd suffered with ulcerative colitis.

I am told that my birth caused more than the usual amount of excitement, as Mum had been very ill from a very young age and was told she would be unlikely to ever have children of her own. However, God in His faithfulness gave her three of us!

It came as an awful shock in December 1979 when Mum was diagnosed with bowel cancer. She had to have surgery and was admitted to hospital. I asked Jesus into my life, to be my Lord and Saviour, at the age of seven but my true walk with God was about to begin and the trust I came to have in God was being sorely tested. This was a difficult place to find myself in, being the eldest and only fourteen. I felt a sense of burden and responsibility heavy on my shoulders, although my Dad and Mum went to great pains never to make me feel that way. I guess it just comes with the territory of being the eldest child!

My memories of that time include lots of support

from different friends and family members. Daily life blended into a messy routine of busyness based around hospital visits and trying to just cope at home with the help of our maid and gardener. I recall being given casseroles by people in the church and I remember one in particular. It was a chicken and mushroom casserole which we served on rice and it was so yummy! Only thing was, there was a lot of it and Dad made sure it lasted for a few meals over a few days! Although very yummy, after a few days I remember feeling like I never wanted to see another button mushroom again! That didn't last too long, as I do like mushrooms now.

My mind was in turmoil. I couldn't quite believe this was happening. The attention on us was nice but it was far too chaotic for comfort. When it dawned on me how ill Mum really was, I swung like a pendulum between moments of panic, wild imaginations and fearful thoughts at how we'd possibly cope without her and yet, at the same time, I felt buoyed by the prayers of family and friends and aware that God was doing something miraculous. When she ended up not needing to have the full extent of radical surgery predicted, there was such a sense of relief and a realisation that God had brought healing and done something that medically hadn't seemed possible. Mum was always positive and filled with joy, even when she was in pain.

Because I was over the age of twelve, I was allowed into the hospital to see Mum whereas Shirl and Jim were not. On the days Mum could get out of bed, she would wave through the window to them in the car park below. I felt so privileged but so sad for them. As a Mum, that must have been so hard for her too.

Frequently, people gathered around Mum to pray for

healing. I can still see her face of courage and her concern for Dad, us kids and others around her. Mum was someone who lived her faith every day. She would boldly share her faith with those around her, she'd smile and welcome people, she went out of her way to make others feel comfortable and she shone Jesus through it all.

There were a few jokes about how people must think she was a very bad sinner since she had so many people come and pray for her! My parents belonged to an interdenominational group of church leaders who supported one another in ministry so, as a result, Mum had many different pastors and ministers coming to lay hands on her and pray.

We'd had a holiday to South Africa planned and Mum insisted Dad still take us children—so in spite of the fact that we were less than keen to go, we went. We camped and trekked through the Blyde River Canyon in the Eastern Transvaal—I remember the exquisite scenery but all I wanted to do was to go home and see Mum.

For me, at the age of fourteen, this was one of my most miserable experiences! I got my period just before we set off and was too embarrassed to tell my Dad who, unaware of my heightened emotional and physical state (I was coping with bad abdominal pain too) tried to convince us this was fun and exciting and had us walking long distances, taking 'short cuts' (long ones really) and all the while I had to deal with no running water or proper toilets as we trekked through some of Africa's most beautiful but quite wild bush land!

For me, it was purely an exercise in endurance and I plodded on just longing for it to end. All the while, resentment and disappointment was building in my heart and I guess I began to feel hardened towards my father's opinions as it felt to me that he would never acknowledge mine. In spite of my constant whinging, I just didn't feel heard. To be honest I must have been an utter pain in his neck! If only I'd had the courage to spell it out and actually tell him the details of why I felt so miserable but we never did share personal details like that and it would have mortified me to do so! I guess a part of me didn't think that telling him why would have made a difference anyway.

Over a few months, Mum recovered well after a few surgeries and life seemed to return to a semblance of normalcy. At this time, Dad was still working for World Vision[1]. This organization utilized much of Dad's past skills and took him into many countries where he saw things, situations and people that no one should ever have to see or live through. Of course, these experiences affected him and he would often come home seeming to be stricter on us and, to me, his opinion was completely irrelevant. It felt to me that he was just getting on our cases more as he sought to bring change and move away from the wasteful gluttony and excess of our 'western' lifestyle.

As I've thought about it, it was quite understandable really, considering that he may have just been helping on a feeding program and witnessed hundreds of starving children with not enough food and medical supplies to go around.

This is easier for me to understand now that I'm

1... World Vision as an overall organization is one of the world's leading humanitarian relief and development agencies. It has offices globally, with projects in many countries of the world, supporting and providing life skills education, basic needs like wells for water, food programs and a child sponsorship program. World Vision holds a non-denominational Christian faith ethic.

older, have children of my own, have struggled to make ends meet and seen his point of view more clearly. But at the time, as a teenager without an acknowledged voice, it felt to me that all he wanted to do was to find something else to criticize and complain about.

Dad has always been thoughtful and often challenged the status quo. His views have been different and often unpopular which I believe can frequently be the case in someone who thinks deeply and looks at alternative viewpoints. Often it is these people who are the world changers. However at that age, I was simply not interested in being criticized and pushed to agree with an opinion I didn't personally hold.

I love my Dad dearly and have had to work through a lot of issues as I've struggled with what it means to honour your father and mother and yet not always need to agree with them on certain topics.

It drove me crazy and hardened me for years to keep hearing Dad's point of view, which honestly differed to mine in many ways. But I see this has been his journey and experience and yet my journey is different. And that's okay. We're not meant to be clones, as we are made different. And we are designed to be a diverse people—all made in God's image—equal, but not the same.

And that doesn't mean dishonour. Honour doesn't mean agreeing with someone on everything but learning how to co-exist in spite of our differing opinions and allowing each other to be who God created us to be, even if that person is doing something in a way we don't necessarily like or agree with.

God has since done a lot of work using a jackhammer on my heart—a heart that had become so hard from feeling unheard, being hurt and feeling criticized—even though instruction and not criticism was the intention. My daily prayer is that God removes the crusty shell that threatens to reform around my heart and that He keeps my heart soft in spite of what happens in life.

5
Kenyan adventures

As mentioned earlier, our family moved to Kenya in 1981. What a visually beautiful place. The cosmopolitan city of Nairobi, the beautiful scenery, wildlife, game parks, tourists, hotels, overflowing African taxis on potholed roads, open jostling markets, unfamiliar smells, heady incense burning, spicy foods, different people and everything unique. With a strong Arabic influence, it is a place of diverse cultures, where East meets West. I see the fascinating differences and beauty now but did not appreciate them then as I longed for familiarity and security. This move (again) was a very painful time for me as I felt so powerless being made to go with my family to a country I was so unfamiliar with. Leaving friends and family and entering a very different culture were difficult adjustments, especially at the age of sixteen.

We lived in a strange mix of culture. We stayed in semi-detached units between an Ethiopian family and a Ugandan family, and I attended a British school and we mixed on weekends with expatriate American missionaries and some of other nationalities too. In some ways, Nairobi was way behind the times. We had no telephone at home and in an age before mobile phones, emails and internet social media, we relied solely on letter writing which could take weeks for a response. This was the only form of communication between my friends in Zimbabwe and myself. Of course, all of this seriously hampered the social life of a sixteen-year-old girl!

Listening to music and reading books were my main source of sanity at that time. I really missed being involved in a Youth Group and basically spent my time hankering for Zimbabwe and life as I'd known it there. Spiritually, I felt as though I'd dried up. My support network of getting together with good friends and learning about God and walking the journey as a Christian in our daily lives, being able to play guitar and sing with my other musical friends—all that was missing—I had no such support. I didn't settle in the church and felt like all I wanted was to be accepted and loved. I struggled at school and where I'd been doing really well at school in Zimbabwe, I began to see my grades slipping lower and my sense of worth plummeted.

And yet, in spite of this dryness, God was there. I still had my quiet times with God, where I would read my Bible and pray even though I didn't really think this made a difference.

I made friends with a girl by the name of Ros who became my best friend. Her parents needed to move to Namibia and to minimize disruption for Ros it was organised for her to come and live with us for a year while she finished her schooling. We were doing our 'O' levels that year. We shared a bedroom and I soon discovered how differently we approached life. She listened to Iron Maiden, Black Sabbath and other heavy music while I listened to Abba, the Bee Gees and lots of other less crazy stuff!

I did have access to some Christian teen magazines which were well worn from being thumbed through!

Throughout our friendship, we would talk on and off about God stuff and, one day, she told me she wanted Jesus to be Lord of her life! That was so exciting and in our room, we prayed and she did just that. What a huge boost this was for my faith! This encouraged me immensely. God heard me and loved me and loved my friend too.

Whilst living there, both Ros and I had the opportunity to climb Africa's second highest mountain, Mt Kenya, with a group of school friends. We loved it but simultaneously disliked the cold, the blisters and the aching muscles.

Only months after moving to Nairobi, Doctors discovered Mum had another cancerous tumour. Again, she spent time in hospital having further surgery and we went through that state of uncertainty again. She recovered well but had become so thin she could wear my younger sister's clothes who, at the time, was about thirteen years old. Through all these experiences and in spite of my hurting heart, I always knew God loved me and heard me. I knew He loved Mum and I was becoming more aware of the fact that He was a miracle worker —where Doctors were saying the worst about Mum's condition and prognosis, God just continually came through and proved them wrong. Mum's health seemed to be improving day by day. I developed a strong faith in God and knew He could be trusted.

In late 1982, Ros left and moved to Namibia to live with her parents. This was heartbreaking and I missed her friendship very much.

The Rhode to Zimkesalia

6
Turbulent times

In early 1983 I left Nairobi, Kenya, and returned to Harare, Zimbabwe. This was my wish; I'd pined for Zimbabwe every day since leaving twenty months earlier. It was a turbulent time leaving my family at seventeen and a half and being put into boarding school when I longed for independence but also longing for family to be near. I was excited to be going home to Zimbabwe but viewed home through what Mum called 'rose-coloured spectacles'— things would have changed but I hadn't realised to what extent. Very soon, the apprehension and anxiety threatened to overwhelm me once again.

During this transition, I always knew that Mum and Dad were praying for me and I'm so thankful for that. Never underestimate praying parents!

The boarding school was like a prison, I felt so lost and lonely and for the first time in my life, was at a point where I actually didn't care if I upset people or did the wrong thing. I was too miserable to care if I broke the rules or caused disruption. The rules of the school were so severe and I was so unhappy.

In recalling this part of my journey, I've realised how the lies of the enemy, labels and fear can dictate how we live and the decisions we make. I was labeled 'rebellious' and struggled with feelings of low self-esteem, insecurity, feeling completely misunderstood, unheard and hurt.

> *A painful time of memories dark*
> *Hurt, lies, deception, isolation*
> *Lonely, afraid, kept apart,*
> *Fear which could grip and taunt*
> *Rejection, rebellion and shame.*

    We were officially only allowed out of the school one weekend in a term and I used that up my first weekend. It was so good to be out of my 'prison' and yet I was filled with dread that I'd have to return. I remember my parents coming from Kenya to Zimbabwe for a holiday and it was during the school term—I think it might have been in April 1983. Because I'd used up my weekend earlier in the year, I couldn't have another and Mum and Dad trying to do the right thing, went along with supporting the school rules. Never mind that I hadn't seen them in four months, I remember them visiting me in the garden at the school for an hour or so then leaving me there as they went to stay with family.
    I sat there and cried, watching them go and feeling like a toddler with my arms stretched out towards them—desperate to leave but feeling abandoned, rejected and hurt. Again, I felt that my opinion was unheard. Or if it was heard, it just didn't matter. I felt ignored.
    This feeling then quite quickly turned to anger. I had moments where I questioned the love of God, my parents' love, the whole of society's 'rules'—I was quite sure that everyone just hated me and was out to make my life a misery.
    As I revisit that year, I know God showed me that He

heard me when I cried out to Him in desperation. In spite of how tossed about by my pain and the hurt I felt, I knew without a doubt that I was anchored to Him, my Rock. Even though it took a while for me to get things back on track, I knew He was there and I knew He heard. I knew, because I'd hear His reassurance in the scriptures I'd read, the ray of sunshine that would shine through the trees, the scent of the flowers as I walked past—I felt His comforting presence.

I believe my parents were honestly trying to do what they believed to be right. They were Godly, upright, law abiding people who followed the rules and upheld the honour of authority. However, there is much more talk these days about what can impact on young people and I don't think anyone knew or realised the impact that the abandonment and rejection I felt that day would have on me. Yes, I had made the decision to return to school in Zimbabwe but as a confused teenager, I was struggling to come to terms with separation and loneliness.

During those couple of years, I was involved in a serious relationship with Rick. Although we were so young and really wanted to do the right thing, we grappled with the natural desires and tension of young people in a relationship. We made promises we couldn't keep, we said things we couldn't have understood at that time in our lives and we got in way too deep. Before we knew it, we were involved in a sexual relationship. I was living with secrets, deception, fear and guilt. I was so unhappy at school and this young man was my lifeline. I was eighteen.

Towards the end of June that year, I had got to the point where I didn't honestly care what those in authority did to me at school—anything was better than the pain

I was in so, one day, I just left. I packed my bags and walked out of the dormitories and got into Rick's car. The next day we drove to South Africa for a few days and I rang my parents in Nairobi from Johannesburg and made it clear I would not go back to school!

For me, this was a radical move—I had been a 'goody-goody' all through my school years but I'd had enough. Spiritually, I was struggling with the whole scenario—I knew I was being rebellious but, at the same time, felt completely justified in my rebellion, feeling as though my parents just didn't care while simultaneously knowing they honestly didn't quite realise the desperate state I was in.

You might ask why they didn't realise how I felt? Well, perhaps it was that, although I had explained and whinged and whined and complained about my situation so much, I had perceived they didn't hear me. Maybe because I had spent years being a whinger, they just didn't take me seriously anymore? I'd been nicknamed 'moaner' by an older relative, which had stung deeply. Perhaps they put it down to 'my age'? I was a hormonal teenager after all!

Much as I tried not to complain, it had become second nature to me and was all I knew for a long time. I felt I had a lot to complain about! As it was, my relatives and parents called me rebellious anyway, so why not live up to my name? I was damned if I did and damned if I didn't, so who cared?

In contrast, as I look back, I know God was definitely with me at this time, even though I went through a stage of not feeling His closeness as much as the conviction of all that I was doing wrong. Somehow though, some way, He held onto me.

It's become very clear to me how careless words spoken over a child or young person can be a curse that 'sticks' until it is cut off in Jesus' Name. I acted out of this curse for years—my default was to find something to complain about and that was always easy to do. Throughout these days and weeks, in spite of outward rebellion, I still communicated with God and His protection was there. After our little trip to South Africa together, we returned to Zimbabwe and I moved into a girls' hostel and started secretarial college, later getting a job in a lawyer's office.

My relationship with Rick began to take a few rocky turns. We broke up, got back together, then after a few months it ended for good. I was working by now and honestly had no direction or sense of hope. I was merely paying the bills—barely! Rick's family had become like mine and our breakup was devastating on more than one level; I'd lost my second set of parents who still loved me but things became more difficult as time went on.

This was a painful period with many unpleasant memories. My heart was broken over Rick. Thoughts of suicide plagued me daily, which frightened me to the core. I would rehearse the ways I could die and who might find my body and what they might think and say. I didn't want to go on; I didn't want to live another day but I knew what I had been taught and I knew right from wrong. I blamed myself and hated who I had become. I had no self-esteem, I felt I was the 'black sheep' of the family, a rebel and the rejected and hated one.

I had always been the odd one out of my peers, cousins, everyone. Not interested in sport or outdoor activities; more interested in music, singing, reading, girly stuff like nail polish and clothes and boys. I felt judged by older relatives and felt less than valuable because I was different. And I was struggling with guilt.

I would spend hours in my room, crying, repenting, asking God to cleanse me and just reading my Bible, feeling condemned and such a sinner, unforgivable and unredeemable. I was depressed, desperate for acceptance and just wanted to die. My heart was broken in a million pieces. I would go to church but then I'd go to nightclubs with friends and try to find where I fitted. At that time, I didn't feel like I belonged anywhere. I went out on dates with quite a few guys, often set up by friends trying to cheer me up, but nothing was right. And I'd lie on my bed and cry until there were no more tears.

In the silence I became aware of God's presence, still loving me, still being my friend, still patient and full of grace. It was this presence of God I clung to—the only shred of hope I had in and through it all. I had my good and bad days but I began to see I would live—I would survive and I would cope and someday it would all be okay. The words I read in God's Word spoke comfort and peace to me.

I'd get up, look in the mirror at my red face, puffy eyes and hair all awry and just sigh! Then I'd tell myself to pick up my game, go and shower, get dressed and pull myself together. Some days this worked, some days it didn't but the gaps between meltdowns and uncontrollable sobbing fits became longer and I began to have hope again.

One day, in late June 1984, I was sitting in the dining room at the hostel where I was staying and I received a phone call from another friend I'd known since I was thirteen years old. Allan and I had been in the same youth group and church, gone to adjoining schools and been friends for years, before I even left for Kenya. The call came from South Africa and he invited me to join him there.

So I did. I packed up and took a long distance bus down to Johannesburg where he picked me up around 10pm at the bus stop. I was exhausted after a long trip and relieved to sit back in his comfortable car. Allan started to pull away and enthusiastically told me we were going to drive to Sun City a couple of hours away, to see the band Air Supply who were playing that night. And we would be meeting friends there! It was by now very late so I just went along for the ride, remembering very little of the whole experience as I slept through most of it!

Our friendship had always been close but never quite close enough for more than a friendship, although the temptation and attraction had been there before. It was one of those things that I guess we wanted to try. Before the wee hours of the morning light hitting the horizon, we decided that we would give a relationship with each other a go but neither of us wanted to ruin the friendship we already had.

We got back to Allan's place early that morning and I fell asleep on the couch. He shared the house with his friend Colin, also someone I'd been friends with and known in Zimbabwe years before but he was more of an acquaintance to me than someone I knew well. A few hours later Al woke me and told me that he had friends coming over for a braai (barbeque).

Lies Vs Truth

You stupid child
You waste of space
You know they're better off without you
How can you be so bad
You know you're unforgivable
You're no good, such a rebel
What would they think if they knew
You shameful girl, you're no good

NO! I love her, the Voice is heard
She is Mine and Mine alone
I've come to rescue, to give life, to free her
I forgive, I love, I offer grace, she is Mine
Hold on to hope dear one, hold on
Don't give up, I will get you through
I love you and I'm faithful
Never mind what people think,
You are loved, cherished
Have hope, trust in Me,
Hold on to My mercy
I will shelter you
Under the shadow of My Wings
You are safe.

Never Give Up

Gasping for breath, I claw
Up, up, I grasp for something
In desperation, I almost stop, give up
Then I feel it
Strength, a hand pulls
Hope rises, courage builds
I gasp for breath again
I rise higher
I breathe, I can breathe
Pulled free, out of the pit
I'm safe.

The Rhode to Zimkesalia

7
New horizons

That was the day my life took a new direction. I met David. He came to the barbeque. It was July 1, 1984. I instantly liked him. He walked in wearing his police-issue long woolen coat, hands deep in his pockets and he nodded his head towards me and said 'hi' as we were introduced. He had the bluest, kind, genuine eyes, short brown hair and a moustache. I noticed he was a quietly spoken man and it impressed me that he was in law enforcement. I soon could see he was a man of good character. I was more impressed when after a little while he picked up a guitar and began to pluck away at those strings, playing some very fine tunes. His hands on those strings were beautiful too, nicely shaped, very attractive and manicured well.

But my mind was so confused; why was I even noticing him like this? It had been a whirlwind decision to leave Zimbabwe and come to South Africa and make it on my own now. I was tired, my emotions were all over the place and I needed to feel loved and heard. I actually didn't really want another relationship but I was so afraid to be alone and here I was having just decided to give a relationship with Allan a go and then I'm noticing David. This just added to my self-loathing.

My relationship with Allan quickly got out of control. We were soon physically involved and this only added fuel to my already low view of myself. Our relationship only lasted weeks as we realised we were really better off just as friends. Allan and his ex-girlfriend decided they wanted to get back together.

At the same time, my attention was being drawn more and more to David and I saw a fair bit of him as he was a good friend of Allan's. All the while I was overwhelmed with confusion. I'd hear the little voices in my head, telling me a bunch of stuff which I now know were lies —'you're useless, you slut, you cheap piece of rubbish, you're pathetic,' and I'd hear God tell me He loved me, He forgave me, He could restore me to wholeness.

I had a choice. In the midst of my confusion, I was praying and asking God for forgiveness, for grace and mercy, for wisdom, for direction and protection. I had to believe He had forgiven me by His grace, He would comfort me, He would direct me. Even in my mistakes and heartache, He was there for me—I could feel His presence. I knew He heard my pitiful cries. He was my anchor.

One thing I have learned is this: God is the ONLY one who will never let us down—He is faithful, He is trustworthy, He is always there and He loves. People let us down. Even people we love and who love us can let us down. People who have authority over us, our leaders can let us down, our families and parents can let us down, our friends can let us down but God never does. We must place our trust and hope solely in Him and know that He is the only One who is totally reliable and trustworthy.

We make huge mistakes but then we have to live with the consequences of those mistakes. However He is still the same, yesterday, today and forever, He is LOVE. He is forgiveness; He brings wholeness to our brokenness and comfort to our pain. God is into restoration and transformation and I am one of those He has restored and transformed.

Through all those hard times, even when I was in the midst of making bad choices, He never left me. When I could feel Him there, when I cried out to Him, He listened. I leaned on Him, I read my Bible, I got convicted by God, felt condemned by the enemy—it was a rollercoaster of knowing that He was my only option of HOPE and yet messing up again, dealing with the shame, living with secrets and going back and asking for forgiveness.

I am so thankful that He didn't give up on me in my immaturity—I also know that my parents' prayers kept me from sliding right down to the bottom of a pit which threatened to swallow me forever. Even though they didn't know what was going on, they consistently prayed and God positioned His angels to protect me, to remind me He was there, to keep me aware of His presence.

Through it all, I kept going back to Him. His Word offered me hope and comfort. I cried over it; the tears fell onto those pages time and again. I can only describe this sense of security in Him as being held fast by my God, the anchor of my soul.

Anchored

Life looms, oceans roar
Storms rage about
Tossed, thrown, tired
Tempted to quit
Give up, sink low
My anchor holds
My hope's in Him, I know.

Unbreakable, immovable
Strong, firm, steadfast
His arm holds tight
Through the dark of night
His love, His promise
He knows it all
My soul is anchored
It is well.

I trust, I cling
In tempests wild
My faith in Him secure
God sent His Son
To save my life
His promise holds,
Of that I'm sure.

Anchored, held,
Sheltered, secure
To trust is what I know
My God is faithful
He never fails
My hope in Him endures.

8
The man, David

I didn't know at this time that David was the man who would become my life partner. At the time I was still staying at Allan and Colin's house, even though Al and I had decided our relationship was preferable as friends. David came over to visit as he quite often did and, during the afternoon, he asked me to go to the movies with him.

So we did, that night. Afterwards, we talked into the wee hours of the morning and within days, I'd poured out my broken heart in honesty to this man who I really hardly knew. I didn't hide a thing. I couldn't believe he listened. He heard me. He knew it all—good, bad, ugly.

The next day he came by again and we went out for a couple of hours for a drive. Lots more talking and he took me to meet his aunt, uncle and cousins who lived a few kilometers away. Within a few short days, we had decided to date.

My heart and mind were in turmoil: excited, happy, ecstatic, scared, terrified and happy again! I didn't want to date for dating's sake—only if there was permanence in mind. So I swung precariously between a wild sense of hope and joy and a chasm of fear.

However, there was something else about David that was a strong force of attraction. Besides the fact that he was a policeman, I could tell he was a man I could trust. Like a rock he was solid, not buffeted about by whimsy and sentiment but reliable, secure, solid, strong, level headed and faithful. He didn't say a lot but when he did, it wasn't trivial, silly, or boastful; it was intelligent, wise and interesting. He had a wicked sense of humour and he made me laugh. I could tell he was gentle and had a sensitivity that showed respect and care.

Within weeks I needed a place to stay as things were beginning to feel uncomfortable with me still staying at Allan's place and so David asked his Aunt and Uncle if I could board with them. They agreed and I moved in. David lived in the police barracks at Alberton, about a half hour's drive away.

It wasn't long before he told me he loved me. Oh he melted my heart—being a man of few words and not given to speaking frivolously, his words went deep into my heart. One thing led to another and before I knew it, I was deep in another relationship that had crossed physical boundaries I'd vowed to myself I'd not cross again. But this was my man and for the first time, I felt really safe.

Along with that feeling though, all my old feelings of guilt began to rise, the feelings of worthlessness, the shame and the self-loathing. And yet, I think a numbness also settled in which frightened me too, as if my conscience didn't seem quite so bothered anymore with the fact that I was sleeping with my boyfriend outside of marriage. Of course, we kept the intimacy of our relationship a secret.

We began to talk of marriage and decided together to get engaged. We bought a ring and made no official announcement but I just started to wear it until people noticed. Dave's Uncle was the first to notice as I played the piano one day and he stopped me, asking if my ring meant what he thought it did. He was so sweet and congratulated us both, telling David he'd made a really good choice!

9

Shock news, nausea and never a day to waste

The news was out and we contacted my parents and told them we planned to get married in June. They were heading to South Africa for Christmas and by now it was September 1984.

I was working, had found a tiny bedsitter flat to rent and had moved into it and become independent.

As the weeks went by, I began to feel like I was coming down with some kind of tummy bug, the nausea and tiredness was overwhelming! It was nearing the end of the year and my work had their end of year closing party for the Christmas break. I sat there with my colleagues and had a few drinks.

I got up from the table I'd been sitting at for a couple of hours, having been handed a few drinks during the course of the afternoon, and I realised I'd had way too much. I felt so woozy and light headed! Thankfully I was being dropped off in town and didn't have to worry about driving. I got out of the car and carrying my high heels in one hand and my handbag in the other, I walked up the block towards the entrance to my block of flats. Outside in the street, was Dave's car—he was waiting for me to come home. As I walked towards him I was quite unaware that I was weaving all over the place until I realised he was watching me and the look on his face was pure fury!

He got out of the car still dressed in his police uniform, having come straight from work, took my elbow and marched me upstairs. He unlocked the flat and ordered me to go and have a bath and pull myself together. He told me that he was very disappointed in me and that it was disgusting for me to be drunk and he wouldn't stand for it! Oh I was mortified—embarrassed beyond belief—and I just cried like a pathetic little girl!

It was a couple of weeks later that I suspected I could be pregnant and we went to the doctor. David waited in the waiting room until our fears were confirmed as I was too embarrassed to have him come in with me. His first reaction when I told him I was pregnant, was to say, "oh shit!" This was very unusual as I'd never heard David swear.

However, minutes later we were in the car and looking at each other with a tidal wave of emotions flooding us both to extremes! We laughed, then we cried, then we laughed again. Well the truth is, I was probably more the one who laughed and cried and laughed again, while David quietly sat there, holding my hand and allowing me to work through my emotions!

Then we looked at each other and realised we had to choose to make this work! I tentatively asked him if he wanted out of our relationship or if he'd choose to stay but I was terrified of his answer! However, he seemed insulted that I'd suggest such a thing. Then he just looked at me and said that this was his baby too and he was going nowhere, that he loved me and was planning to marry me anyway—we'd just move our wedding closer; we'd make this work. Oh thank you God for this man!

Suddenly we had a lot to talk about! We dreamed and planned and freaked out and panicked and dreamed some more. And we laughed, cried, freaked out and settled down again. I did the freaking out more than he did of course! We'd look at each other and not be able to find the words to say sometimes, we were so overwhelmed! We decided to tell my folks when they came to South Africa for Christmas and find a date to move our wedding closer.

My parents arrived in South Africa and it was great to see them again—it had been a long time! I introduced them to David. My family and I were staying with relatives for a few days and I asked if David could stay over one night. They agreed and he slept in a room with my brother.

Early one morning a couple of days before Christmas, I knocked on Mum and Dad's bedroom door and asked if I could talk to them. I then asked if David could come in too. As you can imagine, I very fearfully and haltingly told them I was pregnant and that we wanted to get married sooner than June.

Their faces said it all. They were disappointed and hurt. Their pain was visible, yet in spite of the fact that they were extremely heartbroken for me, they were practical and agreed that we should look at a date much sooner. Straight away, Dad got out his diary and we went to work planning.

I truly thank God for the way they accepted us, loved us and prayed for us, even though I had done the very thing any parent dreads for their child. This was a time of great shame for us both and at the same time, it was very beautiful in other ways.

Of course it was a shock to Shirl and Jim too and I felt their judgment but, somehow, I had to deal with it. That was probably the hardest part and I had to acknowledge that this was something I was going to have to deal with as more people became aware of our situation.

Becoming pregnant three months before we wed and coping with the feeling of having let my family down sometimes threatened to overwhelm me. Having grown up in a very protected and conservative home, I had been taught strong Christian morals and had been a 'preacher's kid'! I knew better. This was a tough time.

But in their wisdom, my parents also knew there was no chance of turning the clock back—it was done; this was real. They loved us through it. So we decided on a date to get married about three weeks later.

During this crazy time, I remember God revealing to me His grace and mercy in a way I had never experienced before. I knew that He loved me anyway, He forgave and He helped me understand that NO baby is a mistake. In Him, there needn't be shame (we all stumble) but in God's grace, we can get up again and keep going. God doesn't use perfect people—none of us are anyway. He uses real people, ones who fall and get up and ones who struggle to keep up. In spite of knowing I need not carry shame, this was something that took a long time to deal with.

I have learned over time that shame is not worth carrying. Yes, I made mistakes—big ones. Yes, I have disappointed God and those who love me. Yes, I stuffed up! I was convicted but not condemned. Holding on to secrets and carrying shame only gives sin power over me and I will not hold that anymore. Some things I am writing about in this book are about me taking back the reigns again—not allowing myself to be robbed for fear of what people might think. The enemy no longer holds power over me and I will live free!

A few days before we married, David's family travelled to Benoni from Cape Town, where they were living at the time. I was so nervous to meet them but I knew they would be quality people; after all, they'd produced David, a man I was so proud to be marrying. We arrived to meet them at David's Aunt and Uncle's house and they smiled and welcomed me as if I was someone they already knew and loved. His sister Gill and brother Andrew were friendly and hugged me, accepting me warmly. I instantly felt a special connection to both David's parents—Margaret and Harold—and particularly Dave's Mum who is like my very own mother to me; I love her as my own.

What a beautiful lady she is! One of wisdom, grace and Godliness. She knew she had to love me because David did and her acceptance of me washed away all the apprehension I felt. Her acceptance of me also made me want to love David the best way that I could, for her sake.

The Rhode to Zimkesalia

10
Choices and commitment

On January 19, 1985, after a whirlwind time of planning—with my parents calling all the shots since we truly had no money and they had to pay for everything—David and I were married at Northmead Methodist Church in Benoni, South Africa.

I wore a borrowed white wedding dress that fitted me a little too loosely and my Mum's string of pearls around my neck. David looked so handsome in his grey suit. My little white veil with the row of artificial roses along the top of the clip was my own and I still have it to this day. My little girl fantasies of getting married and many memories of draping my head in net tablecloths as I played pretend marrying games came flooding in as I got dressed. This was really for real! Yet it seemed surreal.

Our wedding party consisted of three bridesmaids and three groomsmen. The bridesmaids were my sister, my best girlfriend and David's cousin, who all wore turquoise blue frilled dresses that came to just below the knees. Dave's groomsmen wore grey suits and were his old school friend from Cape Town, and two friends from Benoni.

On the way to the church, Dad was so tender in the bridal car. He held my hand and reassured me of his love and that this was an exciting new chapter of my life. I was so nervous and one funny memory I have was that we stopped en route and Dad raced into the corner shop and bought me some peppermints to still my nerves and help me feel more confident—at least I'd have fresh breath! Funny memories!

I remember feeling overwhelmed with thankfulness and love for my parents as I was about to walk down that aisle on my father's arm. This was a big thing! I was getting married! Dad was giving me away to a man he'd only just met! It was big for us both and I knew we were both feeling it. That was precious. I was nineteen.

Nineteen years of being accountable to my parents and I knew I'd not made it easy for them—now I was about to become accountable to someone else, my husband. David was twenty. As I walked down that aisle and looked at him standing at the front of the church, his blue eyes were gentle and loving and in spite of my fears and feelings of uncertainty, I knew I was doing the right thing.

At our wedding reception, we overheard someone say that they gave us a year and our marriage would be over. We talked about it when we got to our first night's accommodation. We were quite annoyed and so both of us made a choice that day to defy that prediction. We chose to honour our vows made before God that day and that we would never throw the word 'divorce' around as a threat; we would live with our choice to stay married.

For me this was a new chapter—a chance to start again. We both knew that life would not necessarily be easy, but we decided to give ourselves and our children to God and do all we could in our power—and God's power—to make things work, even if it got tough.

This is true—that the choices we make at crucial times in our lives have huge consequences. As we both love our music, one of our favourites was a Don Francisco song which had a line that we both held on to: love is not a feeling but an act of the will. This has been something that in reality we have chosen to think on when the froth and bubbles of our relationship dissipated and the sparkles of first love diminished. We made a commitment and we will keep it.

This has not always been easy. There have been times I can honestly say that I considered alternative options. However, as I considered the consequences of any such alternative choice—and the pain we and our families would endure if I chose not to honour our vows—I am now so relieved that I chose to stay. That tough choice kept our family whole.

I remember praying to God to help me fall more in love with my husband when I felt the love waning. He honoured that prayer. In choosing to keep our commitment to one another, we have discovered a love that is deep, true and real and we are truly thankful.

We spent our first night of marriage at a holiday park in a small cabin—nothing flash—and I made sandwiches for our trip the next day. We had about SAR50 to our name which is nothing for two weeks at the beach and petrol too. We started with a full tank of petrol and drove the approximately 600km journey directly to our accommodation in Ballito Bay on the East Coast of Natal, North of Durban. We had been given the accommodation for our honeymoon from David's aunt and uncle.

They were a lazy two weeks. Now living together, as with any newlyweds, we were slowly getting to know each other better.

We pretty much ate what we could afford to make for ourselves in our apartment, which was usually cheese on toast or very simple meals. We splurged one night and had dinner out at a restaurant overlooking the rocks that jutted out into the sea—waves crashing outside while we dined inside, a warm breeze blowing through the open window. I think we had an ice cream cone twice during those two weeks. Such was the nature of our miniscule budget!

Being January, it was hot and humid and not being a fan of hot weather at the best of times, I found it quite uncomfortable. Mostly I was consumed with nausea as I was suffering badly from morning sickness and all I wanted to do was sleep! I remember feeling quite guilty at times, that I wasn't always the best company and I worried that David would wonder what on earth he'd got himself into! Thankfully he was gentle, loving and never complained. He was very supportive.

When I felt well enough, we swam and walked around the area a little. We didn't want to drive anywhere far, as we had just enough money to get home after the two weeks. Consequently, we stayed very close to where the apartment was located, just a short walk to the beach down a side alley.

We had a good laugh one day when we had gone to get the car cleaned and David had meticulously vacuumed all the confetti out bit by bit. It was a warm day and as we drove away from the place where we had vacuumed the car, we turned on the car's air conditioner!

Well, did we get a surprise! We were shocked and horrified, amidst much laughter, that our wedding party had stuffed confetti down every air vent in the car that they could find. And of course, we only used the air conditioner after we'd vacuumed it all up! It came flying out at us at great speed! Boy, did we feel like revenge would be had one day! That little episode kept us giggling for days.

After our two week honeymoon, we drove back and life as a married couple began in my little one-roomed flat in Benoni. What an interesting start.

The Rhode to Zimkesalia

11
Settling, sandpaper and seasons of serenity

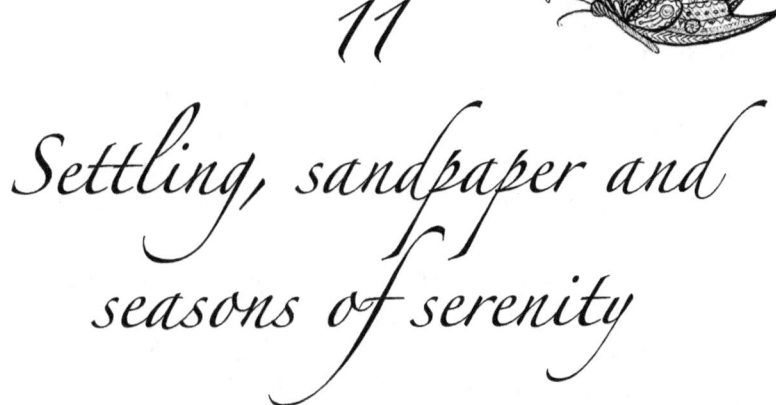

We had been given our double bed by my parents as a wedding present; we had two old retro green chairs which my Grandma had given us, a threadbare Persian looking rug with a very busy design, a bar fridge and an ironing board which David used as a table when he brought work home from the police station. We had a few items for the kitchen and personal effects. Our coffee and bedside tables were upturned boxes with old embroidered cloths I'd been given, draped over them. No washing machine—I hand washed everything in the bath.

Our first couple of years of marriage, we fought. My goodness, we fought a lot! Usually over the silliest things too! Nothing very serious!

For example, neither of us really knew how to cook very well. And for some reason, we just couldn't seem to manage to make soft poached or soft fried eggs. They would break or be hard or not cooked enough or some other issue and we'd take turns to try to get it right but it almost always ended in a fight! One day I said to David

"I think we just won't eat eggs anymore", since getting them cooked to perfection didn't seem like it was ever going to happen!

So we didn't eat eggs for a long time. Then, one day, one of us (I don't even remember who) had another go and perfectly cooked the eggs! And that fight was over! We just somehow got it and realised it wasn't worth the tension. They mostly worked well and sometimes they didn't but we'd learnt to let that one go! Such relief!

Ah, the joys of bringing two entirely different people together and expecting them to co-exist! I've always said that one day I must ask God about this design and plan of his! It sometimes seems too hard!

I think He would smile and say something about us learning to co-exist and being one another's sandpaper, smoothing the rough edges and making us into a thing of beauty; perhaps something about learning to consider another person more highly than ourselves. Hmmm, God's plan. Different to our human thinking and tendencies—His thoughts far above ours. Always with perpetuity in mind.

One tradition we started early on in our marriage, and it's a treat to this very day, is to sit in bed at night with a cup of tea and chocolate and enjoy a chat whilst drinking our tea and savouring our yummy chocolate. It became a time out for us—a cherished sense of home and relief would settle on us and we'd take a breath and feel that we could go another day. After a while, it became a time of deep connection, sharing and prayer too. A great way to end the day.

As the years have rolled on by, we've sure had our highs and lows but as we chose at the start to honour our vows to one another under God, we continue to do so and we have been blessed to have experienced the deepest of loves.

The Rhode to Zimkesalia

12
Building our family

My Mum and Dad, Shirley and Jim moved to Australia a couple of months later and life without close family nearby began for us as a couple.

As I grew in size, I had to face the family and friends who hadn't known I was pregnant—although I know some did, who tactfully said nothing, which was actually worse. Most of them congratulated us and wished us all the best for our future.

We began to build our own family and home life founded on the principle that Christ would be at the centre of it all, no matter what. Well aware of the opinions of others we were acquainted with, especially given my increasing belly, we knew we needed God to help us make it work.

I continued to work for a few months at a company where I was the cash book clerk in the accounts department —it bored me to tears—and David was working shift work between Alberton, Germiston and Benoni. We moved into the police flats in Benoni after a few months, which was wonderful as they were three bedroomed flats and we felt like we had so much space! We did however rattle around as we moved in with our few meagre belongings.

Our finances were very tight and I recall how I'd

count our food items out to make them last the month. I would buy a box of twenty hamburgers which, if we had only one each at a meal, would make ten meals. Then one dozen eggs would give us six meals, having only one each. I would bulk everything out with bread and frozen vegies or, if we were lucky, rice and fresh vegies. A few meals a week were toasted cheese and tomato sandwiches, tinned baked beans or peanut butter and jam on toast. If we had guests over, then I'd make more effort for that meal but it would mean more toast that week for us.

We fell in love with our baby long before he was born and I praise God for a man like David who was so committed and faithfully there for us in every way. For the first time in years, I felt like I belonged.

As the time approached for us to welcome our firstborn babe into our family, we realised we needed to get some baby gear. I honestly don't remember how this happened but, between different family and friends, we were given the basics of what we needed and friends held a baby shower for us, which helped towards getting a few essentials. We were given an old pram with a removable carry cradle and a cot, some clothes, nappies and a baby bath.

As the due dates approached—July 7 was the scan date and July 14 was the doctor's date—it felt like our baby would never come! I wasn't sleeping well, I felt like a beached whale and we were so excited about this little baby's arrival! I had gone to weekly ante-natal classes nearby, with Dave coming to a couple of them too, for about three months prior to the birth which was hugely helpful and helped me to have some vague idea of what I was about to go through!

The day arrived when contractions started. I was twenty and David was twenty-one. He had his clipboard and stopwatch and was timing my contractions throughout the day. I think having a task to do helped David to cope with the whole process. The contractions started around 9am and it was going slow but steady through most of the day. We even visited friends in the afternoon—right in the middle of it! Then around dinnertime, I realised things were getting serious. I hopped in the bath to relieve some of the pain of contractions before we went to the hospital. David sat on a chair in the bathroom and played his guitar beautifully for me, which I loved, and it kept my emotions calm.

We finally headed to the hospital around 9pm at which time labour progressed quite rapidly. The pain was way more intense than anything could have prepared me for and we had been warned of this at our classes. The midwife I had was an older lady, unmarried and had no children, and she ticked me off hugely when she told me it wasn't that bad and not to fuss! I remember asking her how many times she'd been in labour and when she told me she had no children, I told her to shut-up and get out as she had no idea what she was talking about! I was a feisty Mum in labour! About an hour and a half after we arrived at the hospital, our amazingly beautiful baby boy Michael was born at 11.30pm on July 10.

I could hardly believe how tiny he was. He was only 5lbs and within the first few days I had this amazing revelation of the fact that this tiny baby was completely dependent upon us! If we didn't feed, change and care for him, he'd die! The enormity of this responsibility was overwhelming and I struggled with it on and off in those first few months!

All manner of emotions coursed through my being—exhilaration, love, fear, trepidation and exhaustion. David was working shifts so couldn't be there at every visiting hour and my parents were overseas. In a ward of about ten new mums, my baby was the only one who was in the incubator and not in a bassinet next to me. I was utterly overwhelmed. And yet, there was a sense of the deepest love I had ever known that filled me, overtook me and undid me. How could such a tiny, dependent baby cause me to fall so hard in love? It was unreal! I realised that I would do anything at all for this baby—I would give my life for my son, anything at all to protect and nurture him and let him know he was loved and adored.

The day after he was born, I had to have the Anti D[1] via drip as I have a rhesus negative blood type and the young nurse who tried to put the drip in couldn't find a vein. She tried a few times, causing me to bleed all over the sheets—from both arms, so I ordered her to leave me alone. I wouldn't let them give it to me.

A few hours later, a more senior member of the nursing staff, who wanted to know why I was so upset, visited me. After a long chat, I agreed to let them give me this Anti-D just to get them off my back. The much more experienced and gentle nurse came and got it in first time with no fuss. They tried to tell me I'd have problems with subsequent pregnancies if I didn't have it but at that stage I was too emotional and hormonal to even imagine ever wanting more babies! Needless to say, I am of course glad they knew better and insisted.

1... Anti-D (RHO) Immunoglobulin is given to mothers who have a rhesus negative blood group to reduce the chances of antibodies being formed when their rhesus positive baby's blood mixes with theirs at birth, which could then act against any subsequent pregnancies, causing complications.

My memories of hospital had not been pleasant as a child and so being here so many, many miles away from my Mum, having just given birth to my first baby, I felt utterly alone. I was frightened and again a feeling of abandonment threatened to overwhelm me. Of course, it didn't help that the visiting hours were so strict even for husbands and, as David worked shifts, there were days I hardly saw him for more than a minute or two!

We literally had no money. Policemen didn't get paid much. We had no home phone—we would only use a call box and, if we used a relative's phone, we would pay them but it cost a fortune! I couldn't even call my parents to tell them about Michael's birth so we just assumed our relatives would let them know. We received flowers from my parents and a lovely card of congratulations so we assumed they knew our baby had arrived.

After a few days I had a visit from my Uncle. He looked worried. His first question was about Michael. Was he okay? Was something wrong? I felt puzzled and said he was fine, but why? He had had a call from my parents asking if there was any news and had realised they didn't even know he was born yet so he had come to find out why!

Again, I felt so inadequate, like I'd disappointed them, let them down, and stuffed up! The tears would flow frequently during that week and having our darling baby in the incubator was tough. He was badly jaundiced, had to spend a week under ultraviolet lights and came very close to needing a blood transfusion. He took an hour to feed every time and I was told to feed him two hourly. I didn't get much rest!

I read my Bible in bed in the hospital and hung on to any words of comfort that I could glean, knowing deep down that we'd be okay, somehow, with God's help. I swung between valleys of deep self-pity and the knowledge that I was now a mum and I had to look after my baby as well as I knew how. I had to let the self-pity go, I had to choose to grow up and be the adult here. I had to learn some decorum, some grace—I didn't really know what grace was yet. In actual fact, I still felt like I wanted to run into my mum's arms and be comforted by her and let her handle the grown up stuff.

This was my life. My choices had led to these consequences. I had to make it work and so, with a steely determination, I decided I would have to do just that!

Being a strong and independent person, I have had to battle the desire to make life work my way or choose to let God take over, submit and allow Him do things His way! That has not been easy, yet I have learned over time, with many ups and downs along the journey, that it is always much easier to surrender to God instead of insisting stubbornly to do as I please. His ways are higher than mine.

During my pregnancy, I had been careful not to gain too much excess weight and had gained only seven kilos in total. On the day I gave birth, I lost eleven kilos and continued to lose weight as I breast fed my son. Even though I ate a lot, my body continued to lose weight until I got down to forty-five kilos by the time Michael was about six months old.

David had to go to the border for further police training and to man a post there, for supposedly three months during Michael's first few months. Thankfully, he was only gone about six weeks. This was due to my desperate call to the Chaplain and a doctor's recommendation. The doctor was concerned about my stress levels, coping on my own as a new young mum with a very limited support network and he said I was anorexic, which I didn't believe as I knew I ate well and never vomited. Whatever the reason, my pleas were heard and David was soon home again, much to my relief!

    Life as a young mum was hard. It took us two months (with a tiny baby) before we could afford to buy a twin tub washing machine, so I hand washed everything. We didn't have disposable nappies either. Without a tumble drier, cloth-towelling nappies were strewn over anything I could find to dry them. The oven set to low temperature had nappies hanging over the open door, the dining room chairs, the clothes rack, anything! If the weather was good, I would take the lift up the eight or so storeys to the top of the building, with Michael sitting in the pram and a basket of washing on my hip and hang it on the clotheslines on the roof.

    We still had no home phone (and there were no mobiles then) so if I needed to make a phone call I would have to go downstairs to the lower level and use the payphone—which invariably had someone using it and someone else waiting in line. I would have to join the queue. It was situated next to the ground floor lift, just under cover but exposed to the wind and cold, near the car park. Not the safest place to stand and have a chat. David had the one car, which he drove to work. I had the pram and would go out walking often, just to get out of the flat.

    I was painfully skinny, we didn't have much money, my ill-fitting clothes hung on me and I would push Michael in the pram from bin to bin, retrieving glass bottles which I could return for a ten cent deposit at certain corner shops. With this money, I would buy bread or whatever was most needed at the time. I look back at those days and remember the humiliation: looking around me, trying to see if anyone saw me taking those bottles out of bins, being embarrassed that I looked the way I did—so skinny it was ugly.

Although I was twenty, I looked much younger and one day when I was pushing Michael down the sidewalk, someone told me I was such a nice big sister taking my little brother out for a walk and helping my mum! I just smiled and didn't bother to tell them this baby was my own. I hated the judging looks and assumptions.

I have become aware of how culture, era and opinion can play a big part in how different generations parent, raise their children and discuss life issues.

As a young Mum, I received so much advice from so many people, in so many places I found myself in. Comments like: 'Don't spoil him—he'll expect to be cuddled and he'll wrap you around his little finger, so don't hold him too much—put him down and let him cry it out, he'll soon learn who's boss'; 'Don't use a dummy'; 'Oh honey, why won't you give him a dummy'; 'Never put him to sleep on his back, always on his tummy, you don't want him to choke on his vomit'; 'Babies need to have water too, so make sure you're giving him boiled water in between every feed'; 'he's so little, make sure you feed him every three hours on the dot'; 'don't demand feed, he'll think he's in charge and become very demanding'; 'demand feeding is best, baby knows when he's hungry and how much he needs'; 'oh he's already one year old and not out of nappies yet'; 'Why haven't you potty trained him'; 'I had all four of my boys trained by the time they were one'; 'Don't train him too early, he'll be psychologically damaged, he must be ready for it himself'; 'Breastfeed only'; 'Top him up with a bottle, he's hungry'; 'make sure you feed baby on both sides'; 'only feed one side at a time, drain one breast completely so baby gets foremilk and hind milk'. Oh it went on and on!

I will never forget my husband's Aunt giving me some different and wise advice: She said 'Cathy, you'll hear a lot of advice in your life but he's your baby and you know him best. Listen to the advice, think about it and then do what you think is best.' Oh what wise words—I've often thought of those words as I've navigated through my parenting journey.

One thing I have noticed in being a daughter and being a Mum, is how differently generations can speak into their children's lives. In my childhood there was more emphasis on talking about any educational achievement and doing well academically than there ever was on being the best person you were created to be, including emotionally and mentally.

I knew I would be praised for doing well at school or gaining some qualification but who I was without that qualification was highlighted as having a damaging impact on my future. It seemed to me that what was seen was more important than what was not seen. I interpreted this as me being second rate if I didn't have some kind of degree or recognised qualification.

I don't think the impact of this was ever thought through by most adults of that time or my parents—they only wanted what was best for us but I think it was a cultural and generational norm back then. As a result, I compared myself poorly to my siblings for years. They'd both earned degrees and I hadn't.

I was also always self-conscious of my looks. A

skinny kid with wispy, fine blonde hair, freckles and such fair skin I couldn't tan, I didn't feel pretty or beautiful in any physical way. Of course, being a late developer didn't make me feel like I fitted in either! Mum would talk about beauty needing to be deeper than skin deep, which is right, of course, and I think the fear of encouraging vanity kept physical compliments to a minimum.

In an effort to ensure my kids feel loved no matter what, I have tried to make sure they feel loved simply because they are who they are. I have called them gorgeous and beautiful and all kinds of names that I've tried to pick which are encouraging and uplifting and point more to who they are than what they look like or do. I am not concerned about vanity, as they are intelligent enough to know that real beauty comes from within.

As a parent, I am sure their impression of this might differ and they could think of times when it hasn't felt that way for them. Of course, there have been the fun nicknames and normal family fun times of teasing and nonsense which is all a part of family life! I too, am an imperfect parent and it's a tough gig!

As a Mum, I have taught each of my children that their value is profound. My prayer is that, no matter what the external influences are, they will find their value in who they are in Christ—nothing else. They are created in God's image.

Cathy Scott

Motherhood

Persistent wails pierce that semi-conscious state
As awareness of the need becomes apparent
Groggy, semi-awake, I retrieve first born
And attach to meet the need ...
first silence, then gulping
The child is satisfied and settles with relief
I doze, head pounding with lack of sleep
To face another day of repetition
Keeping up with demands, needs, life
Tripping over washing and misplaced toys
Mingled moments of pure delight and joy
Wiping sticky fingers,
Kissing tears on dirt smudged cheeks
Tiny arms wrapped around my neck –
I can live on those for weeks
Sweet seconds of peace
interspersed with frantic survival
The milestones, mess and mountains of work
So tired I barely function
Some days a lack of gumption
And yet, such love, it fills, joy overflows
The sacrifices, sleeplessness and sorrows
Make way for memories,
minutes irreplaceable, moments to cherish

And fast the years go by, time so does fly
And more needful children arrive
With joy and love, no money can buy
These little ones, formidable, rapturous

The agony, the ecstasy, so fast they grow
Demanding to know, their wants, their needs
Their individuality, so unique in advancing maturity

Those teen years are tough, actually quite rough
Angry words, misunderstandings, rejections
Doors slammed shut, rolled eyes and silence
Boundaries being broken, testing just token
These days make you long for those long teething nights
When it seemed so hard but then your will overcame
Now these ones have wills and independence is gaining
Triumphs and failures and victories and laughter
All part of family dynamics together
But here ever after I live with heart on my sleeve
For these kids who were tethered to me – ties so strong
They get cut and yet soul ties stay true
To my children I say, I will always love you.

On up and down trail, this life I'd not trade
The moments of love, whispered prayers, desperate pleas,
To raise these precious ones cannot be compared
This is life, rich and full, pained and tired, sacrifice more
Little people grow large and transform
And my soul it loves it all
Sings with joy at their successes
Aches with pain at their losses
But always it yearns and swells with gratitude
For the opportunity and privilege to mother
These offspring, my treasured possessions.

The Rhode to Zimkesalia

13

Our first family holiday

In late 1985, David and I decided to have a holiday with Michael who was by now six months old. David wanted to take me to Cape Town, where he'd grown up, to show me his home and introduce our little boy to friends and family there.

I wanted so badly to be the perfect wife and make a lovely cake for Christmas time so I did and we adorned it with the perfect fondant icing and piped decorations. We worked for a few days together, to get it right, and it was such fun! We iced that beautiful fruitcake and spent hours getting a star template just right.

We decided to travel at night as the long trip of approximately fifteen hours would be easier with Michael sleeping for most of it, so we packed up and at the last minute we took the cake to the car and it fell! Ooops! The icing, which had hardened, as it should, just shattered and broke, and we felt so devastated! All that work, shattered on the ground in pieces! It was heartbreaking! Oh well, we decided we'd just re-do it when we got there and proceeded to drive from Benoni to Cape Town, with the bits in the cake tin and some extra icing ingredients and tools.

That was a funny trip! Firstly we had packed up the VW Golf to the hilt with Michael's bassinet cradle tucked in tight between luggage and guitars and the cake! In those days, we didn't have baby car seats and when Michael wasn't sleeping, he sat in my arms for the trip! When he needed to be fed, I'd breast feed in the front seat! How times have changed!

We had a lovely two weeks there, with David showing me all his old haunts and driving me up to show me the lookout points which showed off the beauty of this old port city.

Unfortunately we had a bit of a disappointing experience when David so carefully spent a whole evening up the side of Table Mountain, with his camera on his tripod, getting time delayed shots of the city lights on the night before we had to leave. Only later, did we realise he had no film in the camera and had spent the whole night wasting time! Many a laugh and embarrassed and frustrated chuckle was generated from that unfortunate experience!

However, it was a lovely trip and very special getting to know Dave's family better and letting them enjoy getting to know Michael too.

14

Overseas travels

Over a three month period in late 1986 and early 1987, my parents made it possible for us to visit Australia for a holiday and we had a lovely time with my family.

My Dad had an old Chrysler which fitted us all in and we did some great sight seeing in Victoria and South Australia. Many photos taken of that visit bring back the memories! We toured quite a few areas, catching up with old friends who we'd known from Zimbabwe days. There was lots of driving, fun and special family times. During that time we decided we would look into moving to Australia sometime down the track, in maybe five years' time.

On this holiday, we decided to try and grow our little family. I fell pregnant with our second baby. We were so excited and anticipated her arrival with a new enthusiasm, feeling as though, this time, we were not being judged like we had been the first time around. It was good to know our little family was growing.

The Rhode to Zimkesalia

15
Family expansion

In September 1987, I gave birth to our precious daughter, Megan. Oh the joys of a little girl—words could not describe! So in love we were again! And of course, thrilled to have one of each gender. Big brother Michael adored his baby sister too!

We'd started our lives together with so little, and still we didn't have much, but God provided for our needs and we were flourishing as a family. By now, David had left the police force and was working for a computer company. We had also moved out of police accommodation into a two bedroomed flat in Benoni.

We were members at our local charismatic Presbyterian church and, as we became more involved, we grew in our faith and in our conviction that God was our rock and anchor.

Earlier in 1987, before Megan was born, David's family had moved from Cape Town to Benoni. It was great to have them living near us and to enjoy being a larger family unit. It was precious to get to know my Mother and Father-in-law and Gill, my sister-in-law, and Andrew, my brother-in-law. It was special to have family close and we cherished them.

In 1988, we moved into our very first house! It was small, had only two bedrooms, but was on a new estate and was a compact little place, clean and fresh! A rental still, but we were no longer in a flat and we had a little land, with room for Michael to ride his scooter around and to kick a ball with his Dad!

I discovered I loved to be a 'homemaker' and decorated with much enjoyment. I picked fabric to make curtains and my small kitchen and dining room shone cheerfully in bright yellow checks. It felt like we had a real home, a real family and I was happy!

Within a year however, we were moving again! With the help of David's aunt who was a real estate agent, we were able to invest in buying our very own first home, only 2km from our first rental house!

We now had three bedrooms and again I decorated with all the old fashioned enthusiasm of older generation mums, including my own. I regularly had fresh cut flowers in vases—sometimes from my very own garden! What joy! And when I'd cooked a nice meal and the bed was made and the washing was out, nothing made me more pleased! I felt like a real mum, a real wife and it helped to validate me!

What I didn't realise then was that I was beginning to enjoy the satisfaction of design and display, even though for years it never eventuated until I formally practiced and studied interior design.

Being able to excel in this area is not easy with young children who throw things out of toy boxes at crazy speeds and fling them across the room even when you've just tidied up!

I began to notice, when older relatives commented on how well we had done for ourselves, that I felt good. A sort of pride and sense of achievement came over me that I liked! Having started out our lives together when we were so young and covered in a cloak of shame and stigma, I guess I subconsciously felt we had to prove ourselves worthy of being able to have a good marriage and raise our own healthy children. It was as if I needed people to know we could do it—that we weren't complete failures!

As I have gotten older, I have realised that those people's comments have affected me for years. I have felt good and validated when my house is tidy and my home is homey and my life seems to be in order—at least when it looks that way I feel better. The reality, as I have come to realise, is that no-one has it all together. The house can look amazing but it doesn't mean things are all good! In the same way, the house can be messy but there can be lots of joy and laughter.

We are all so good at hiding behind masks and yet we need to be more real with one another. I still like my house tidy, by the way, as it helps me think more clearly! I like it for the satisfaction it gives me. But I am a lot less worried if you see it messy now—my home's presentation is not who I really am and if it's a total mess, much as I still don't like it, I'm okay with that. It doesn't define me.

Settling into this house was fun. We put up a front fence and got two puppies. We had a Labrador and a Golden Cocker Spaniel. We also had a lovely tortoiseshell pussycat. I grew a few of my own vegies and planted some flowers. Some didn't last too long as the dogs did love to dig them up!

Photo Gallery

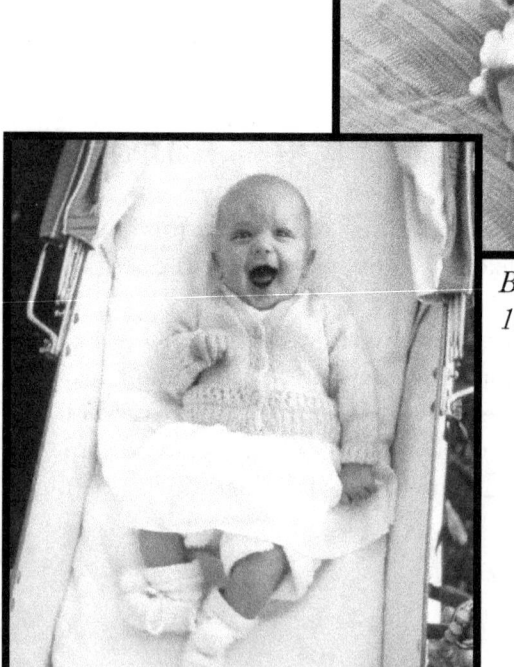

Bonnie with Cathy, 1965, Rhodesia

Cathy, 1965, Rhodesia

Cathy, 1970, Rhodesia

Cathy, 1972, Rhodesia

David visiting me at my flat, 1984, Benoni

David, 1984, Benoni

David and Cathy, 1984, just engaged, Benoni

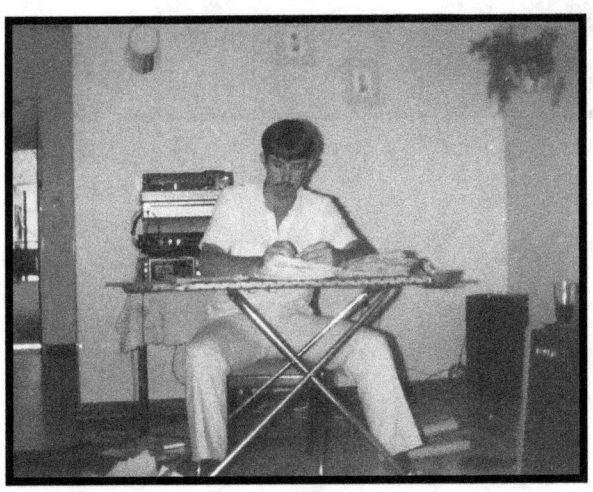

David working at our makeshift ironing board desk, 1985, Benoni

Our Wedding Day, 19th January 1985, Benoni—Gill, Harold, Bonnie, David, Cathy, Peter, Margaret, Jim, Shirley

Our Wedding Day, 19th January 1985, Benoni

Our Wedding Day, 19th January 1985, Benoni

Out little family grows, 1985, Benoni

Cathy and Michael, 1985, Benoni

Cathy, 1985, Cape Town

David and Michael snoozing, 1986, Benoni

Bonnie and Cathy with Meg, 1987, Benoni

That 80's look! Cathy and Meg, 1988, Benoni

Cathy, Mike and Meg, 1988

Cathy, Mike and Meg, 1989

Siblings: Cathy, Shirley, Jamie (Jim), 1993, Melbourne

Re-united with family: Shirley, Dad (Peter), Jim, Mum (Bonnie), Cathy, 1993, Melbourne

Mum (Bonnie), 1995, Melbourne

Jim, 1996, Australia

David and Sarah, 1995, Melbourne

Sarah's birth with both grandparents able to visit! Margaret, Sarah, Cathy, Bonnie, Peter, 1995, Melbourne

The family expands again, 1995, Melbourne

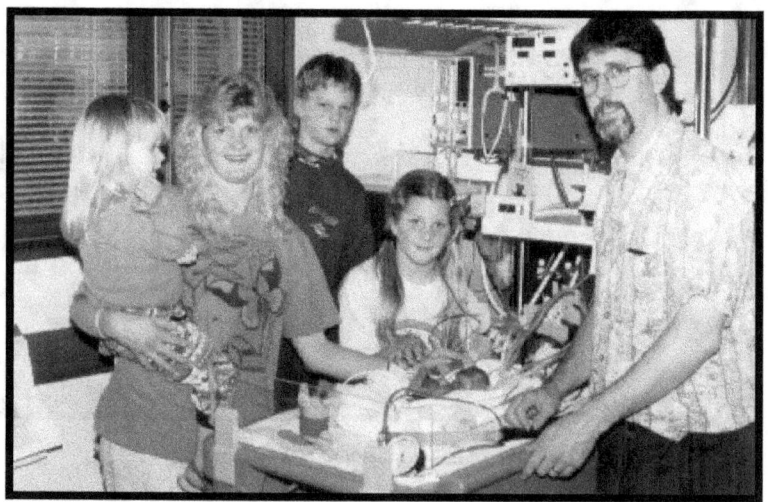

Together with Jesse at Monash Hospital, 1997, Melbourne

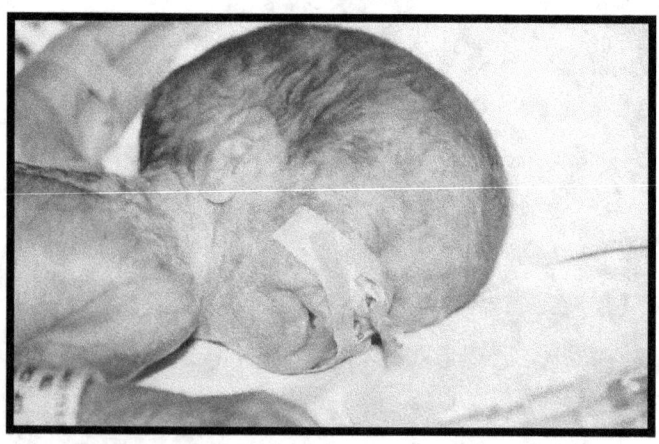

Jesse Iain, Neonatal Intensive Care Unit (NICU) Monash, December 1997, Melbourne

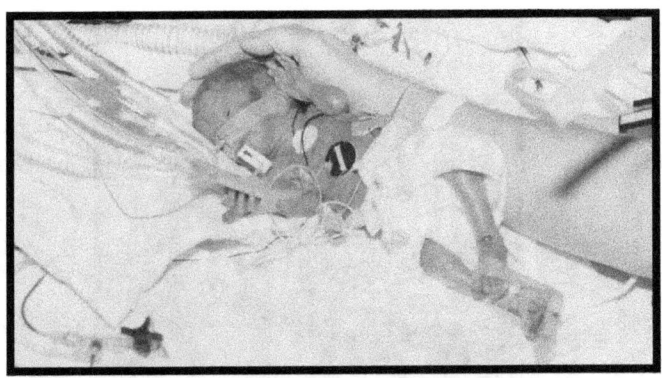

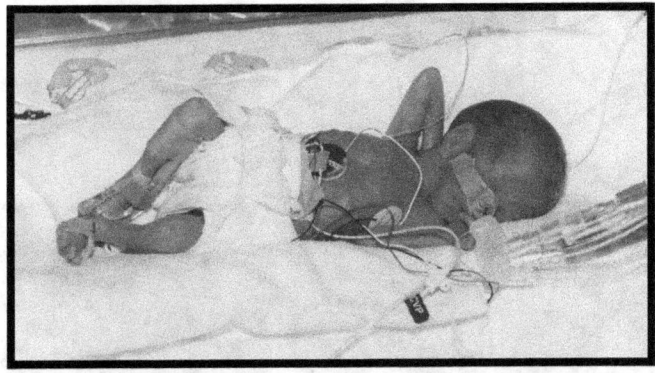

Jesse's Memorial Plaque at Lilydale

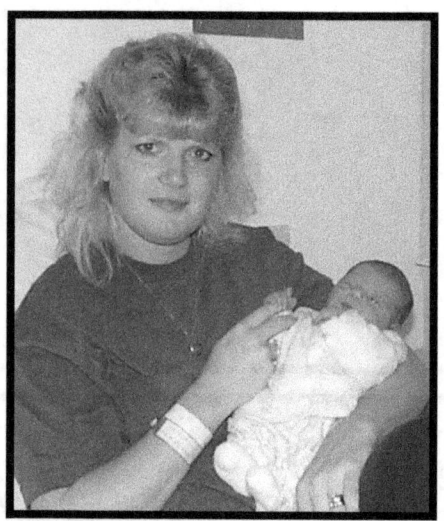

Cathy and Joshua, 1999, Melbourne

Our family, 2009, Melbourne

David and Cathy, 2015, Melbourne

The Rhode to Zimkesalia

16
His dad, my mum and an imminent move

During late 1990, David's Dad became unwell and was diagnosed with lung cancer. He'd never been really healthy since I'd known him, as he'd suffered two strokes, was diabetic and had angina. He was given possibly a year to live, so it was with much shock when I received a call in late March from Gill that Dad had passed away peacefully in his chair next to the bed, after only three months since diagnosis. I rang David at work and asked him to come home as I needed to talk to him urgently. He being the loyal worker he is wouldn't just leave work unless I told him why. So I did. I felt so awful. The phone went silent and then he said he was on his way.

My Father-in-law loved music, sound production, a good joke—and anything SWEET! What a naughty man! He'd worked for the South African Broadcasting Corporation (SABC) for many years and had some of their old equipment that he spent much time tinkering with. We loved him dearly and a few hours after he'd passed away, Andrew commented that Dad was probably mixing sound for the angels! Laughter in the midst of sadness is such a release!

He had only recently given his heart to Jesus, which was a precious relief and provided a lot of comfort for the rest of us in the family. He was sixty seven. One of Dave's Mum's favourite songs, which Dad loved too, was sung at his funeral and came to mean so much to me.

We got a fresh revelation that choosing to hang on to God in the midst of pain was what we needed to do.

Because He lives, I can face tomorrow
Because He lives, all fear is gone.
Because I know, I know, He holds the future
And life is worth the living just because He lives.[1]

The words of this song have blessed me countless times, as I have sung them over and over in the depths of pain.

Whilst still living in South Africa I received a phone call from my Mum in 1990 that her cancer had returned and she needed immediate surgery. I sank to the floor in tears and wept. An overwhelming memory of what we'd gone through years before came over me and I wondered if she would pull through again this time, or if this was it.

Michael, aged four at the time, was worried and came to cuddle me and ask what was wrong. I told him Granny was sick. A very affectionate child with a big heart, he encouraged me and wrapped his arms around my neck in a tight hug. Then off he went to his bedroom and closed the door. A few minutes later I went in and found him on his knees next to his bed praying. Oh my heart ached with love for this boy. He looked sincerely into my eyes, pushed the hair away from my face with a

---

1... Because He Lives - chorus by Bill and Gloria Gaither © Copyright 1971 William J. Gaither, Inc. All rights controlled by Gaither Copyright Management.

gentle touch and again kissed my tears, reassuring me that Granny will be okay because he'd prayed and asked God to heal her. The faith of a child!

Within a day Mum was in surgery and after an ileostomy, began to recover well. She and Dad visited us in South Africa only months later and it began to stir in us a greater desire to pursue a life in Australia.

Along with the joy and excitement of being able to live nearer my family so my parents could know their grandchildren was a cloud of uncertainty, especially regarding my Mum, as it was becoming clear, bar a miracle, wouldn't have many years left. Old memories began to raise their ugly heads. Fears of losing friendships, of starting again, being the odd ones out and not fitting in, were surfacing and I had to intentionally push them away.

However, this time I had my husband and children and we were a unit. We were not alone and would make this move together. Spiritually we had grown much closer to God and one another and I had prayed much about this since our first visit to Australia as I had become aware that something this big was often to blame for broken marriages, financial dire straits and such. This was why for a few years I'd not said much, understanding this needed to be something we both agreed upon. I'd prayed instead for five years. Eventually after my parents' visit, emigrating was something that David had suggested we look into again. I did a silent happy dance inside!

Having recently been in a church service where a guest speaker had prayed over us, we felt God's confirmation. The speaker didn't know us at all and God gave her a 'picture'. She told us that she didn't know what it meant but that all she could see was a vast landscape with a huge red rock in the middle of it. To us, this confirmed that we should pursue our desire to move to Australia as one of its most famous landmarks is Uluru in the centre of the continent (then known as Ayer's Rock).

17

And we're off! — to resettle and adapt

September 1991 saw us emigrating to Australia. We applied in April and the two kids and I were in Melbourne by September 11 of that year.

It was a process, which in our case defied the norm, in that it took many people two years or more to be approved by the Australian Immigration Office. We had to fill in hundreds of forms, apply for passports and visas, have police checks—from any country we'd lived in during the previous decade, which for me was three—medicals, aids tests, all sorts of other tests; we needed letters of compassion from my Mum's doctors documenting her medical history, also from my brother's doctors (as he'd had open heart surgery in his teens twice) and they had to fill out forms saying they'd be our sponsors for two years.

All up there were 186 documents we had to have cleared and current before we even submitted our application! Then we had to be interviewed. There was insurance as well and we had to itemise everything we took with us and that wasn't much! Even so, itemising cutlery can become tedious when going through everything so finely!

A faith exercise began as we sold almost all we had and camped in our house before we sold it, just to be able to buy our tickets to come to Australia. We slept on mattresses on the carpet, surrounded by a few boxes and suitcases as we packed and prepared. We received some criticism from some people who thought we were crazy but we felt strongly that it was right and God was directing us to Melbourne.

We ended up getting our visas only ten days before me and our two children got on the plane to come. It taught us that God's timetable is not dictated to by our desires. God is never early or late. His timing is perfect.

As we sat on the runway, about to taxi out for takeoff, my heart ached as I looked out of the window at this beautiful land of Africa and wondered when, if ever, I'd be back. And it was hard, because I was with the two kids and David had to remain behind to wrap everything up before he could come over too. Feelings were very mixed as tears trickled down my face, farewelling my home and yet excited for what adventures lay ahead. I held Michael and Megan close as we gathered speed on that runway and lifted off and rose into the sky heading for Australia.

We arrived in Melbourne in September 1991, just in time for my sister Shirley and Glenn's wedding. Dave followed two months later in November after the house settled and he wound things up at work.

I was so relieved to be in time for such a special occasion. I was maid of honour and Michael and Megan were pageboy and flower girl. Our clothes and shoes had been acquired before we arrived and we had some hilarious laughter when my shoes didn't quite fit and were a bit big! It was very special seeing my family again and my little sister who was getting married! Wow! She looked like a princess, so beautiful, poised and confident and she shone with joy and love!

It was so precious too, to see my little brother who was now so much taller than me, towering over us all at 6'4". He was a larrikin and it was fun getting to know him again.

Jim was a bit of a hippie, with his free spirited choice of clothing—not much matched, odd socks if he wore them at all—and his ginger sprinkled unruly head of curls, knotted leather bands around his wrists and a shark tooth pendant around his neck. A part of me couldn't take my eyes off this handsome young man who was my brother and I was trying to process five years of not seeing him, during which time he'd grown from a boy to a man.

He was such a mischief and on our way to the rehearsal the night before the wedding (only two days after I'd arrived in the country) I went with Jim in his car. Suddenly at a red light, he gave me the fright of my life when he opened his door, got out and ran around the car behaving like he was a gorilla, making all the noises, fist punching his chest, and hammering on the car bonnet! Then just as the light turned green, he hopped back in and drove off!

I sat there in shock and just laughed and laughed and laughed! How precious to have time to get to know my crazy brother again—how very special. Five years of not seeing Jim was a long time. He was about nineteen at this stage. Shirley's fiancé Glenn wasn't shy either and I was quite surprised to meet this fun loving, outgoing young man who would become my brother-in-law. I was so happy for Shirl.

The wedding was beautiful and Godly and I couldn't help but notice the difference between my rushed wedding years before and Shirl's beautiful celebration of marriage and once again I began to compare and came up short. This insecurity had plagued me for many years until I realised that God had made us different; I was no less of value to Him than anyone else and we were equally loved.

God was so good in the years following. Michael started school in October 1991 and did a term of prep, being so over-ready for school that the following year he continued on into Grade 1 and excelled.

David arrived in November 1991 and began his search for work. At the time I was working in the city of Melbourne for a loss adjusters firm and it kept us going. We stayed with my parents for seven months, until we found a place to rent not too far away. David had work by now and we began to set up home again.

This was all a very special time. We had space as an extended family to enjoy being together and for Mum and Dad to get to know their grandchildren while we were settling into our new adopted land.

We adapted well, made new and close family friends and became involved in a very special Baptist church, where after a few months, I was offered part-time work in the office which I did for a few years.

This church was like family to us. Throughout our time as members of this church, God matured us and we learnt how to be a family who didn't just go to church out of duty but because we knew it was God's desire and we loved it. One of our strengths learnt back then was to turn up, be involved, support what was happening and make what we did count for something good and worthwhile. We had great leaders who believed in us, didn't judge us, taught us and as a church the people there helped us to assimilate into the Aussie culture to a large degree. Of course, we will still always be African at heart.

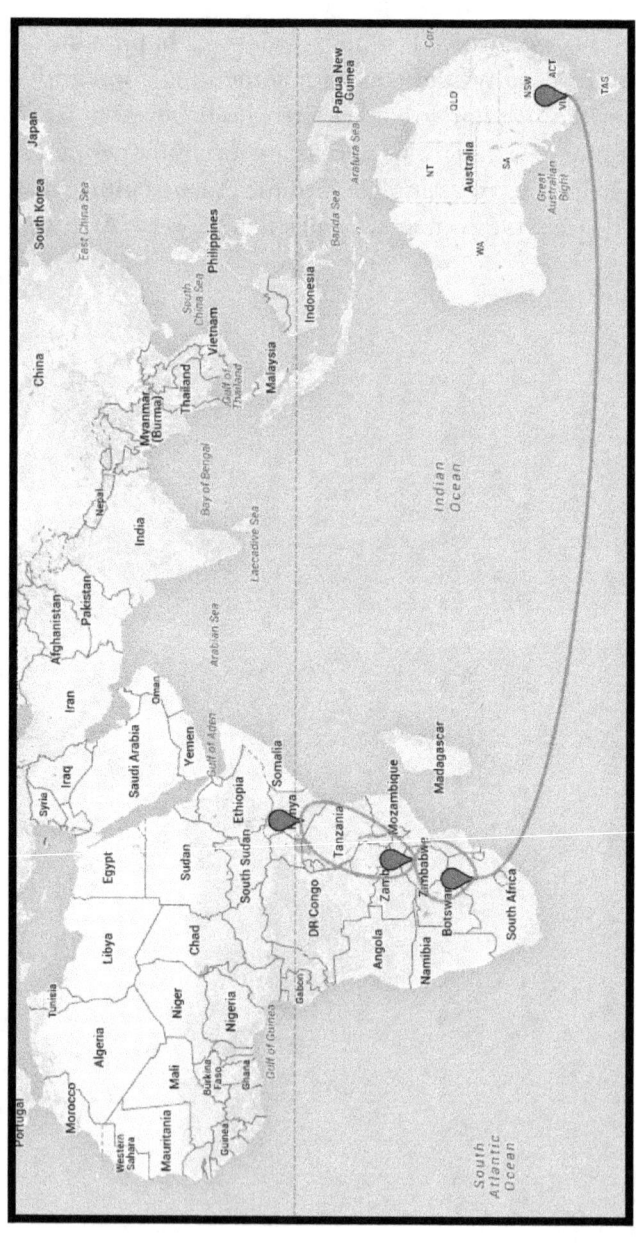

18

Trusting in the tough times

In late 1993, with some sadness, we said goodbye to my Mum and Dad, who moved to the Solomon Islands with World Vision, for what was supposed to be a two year secondment. Mum's health had improved a fair bit but she still had to be careful and wasn't strong. She was amazing; she would never let her health stop her from supporting Dad in his role within World Vision and backed him even when it was difficult for her. Dad on the other hand was very sensitive and gentle with Mum and we were so thankful for his love for her.

One morning in October 1994, as we prayed in the church office during devotions, I felt God speak very clearly to me. He said, "Trust in me, Cathy, for I know the future." I didn't hear his audible voice but I heard this sentence in my head and realised this came from Him. It was so clear and repeated again and again. I could see there was truth in this encouraging reminder but I was puzzled as life was just great and all was well as far as I knew.

I told David about it and we began to pray that God

would grow our trust and faith in Him and that whatever would come our way, whatever He was preparing us for, we'd be strong enough, in Him, to do as He said and choose to TRUST Him—choose to believe that He held our future in His hands.

Only a couple of weeks later, we received news that Mum was returning to Australia with a suspected flare up of the cancer again. Dad followed a few weeks later, since he had to pack up their home in Honiara once the diagnosis was confirmed.

The timing of this return of my parents to Melbourne was challenging. They didn't have a home here as they planned to buy again when they returned, and so they arrived to stay with us—just after David's Mom and sister Gill arrived from South Africa for a visit with us too so we had a full house—even fuller when Shirley and Glenn and Brendan, their first child, came down from Kyabram to spend time with us all! To add to the chaos, I was only weeks away from giving birth to our third child!

Those couple of months with David's family and my parents staying with us were very special but full of mixed emotions. On one hand we wanted to spend time light-heartedly sightseeing with our overseas relatives but, at the same time, Mum's illness was serious and tending to her needs was priority.

Daily life was super busy and it was a hot summer! The months of December 1994 and January 1995 were quite overwhelming, all the more as I was so close to giving birth. I recall not being able to sleep and doing the ironing in the lounge room at 3am with the television on very softly and fans whirring to keep me cool. With such a houseful, it seemed to become an endless round of feeding the five thousand, doing the washing and doctor's visits.

It was confirmed that the cancer was now in Mum's liver and pretty much everywhere else. Mum underwent chemotherapy and was given only a short time to live—we didn't know how long.

I went into Mum's room one afternoon and she was lying on her bed in tears. I wept with her and we prayed. She was so amazing. Her faith shone through her pain even when she expressed her human fears of how soon and how much pain she'd die in. She was so honest and open with me, I felt so honoured. She didn't try to hide where she was at and, although so painful, I was glad she was human too. She spoke words of wisdom and care and concern for us, her family. She didn't want to burden us at all. Even in her pain, she was caring for us all.

It was clear that Dad was already deeply grieving Mum's loss and it was heartbreaking to see. We tried our hardest to ease his pain and be sensitive amidst the daily life stuff—chemo, house hunting for them, my two lively kids and overseas relatives. This was a difficult time for all.

Mum and Dad had been married 31 years in January 1995, so they decided to celebrate a special anniversary occasion with family and friends at the church where they fellowshipped. It was a significant evening for them and us all and, knowing that time was short, made it all the more poignant.

I mentioned I was pregnant with our third child at this stage and our second baby girl, Sarah, was born at the end of January. Again, we fell so in love with our baby, as did her older siblings, Michael and Megan. In some ways it was like starting again, since we'd had a seven year gap and in some ways it was second nature to me. It was so amazing and I loved the whole experience so much! Being older and a little wiser certainly made it much easier!

It was also such a joy to have a baby with all my family there—we hadn't had that luxury with our first two in South Africa. In addition to having David's Mum, it was extra special for us to have my parents and a chance for my Mum who could enjoy one of her grandchildren being born nearby and being able to love on Sarah at such a young age. I have precious images in my mind of Mum rocking Sarah to sleep whilst singing or humming to her. These images are burnt into my memory forever.

Mum was an amazing Grandmother. She took time to read and play games with Michael and Megan and steadfastly prayed for them. They loved her.

We knew time with Mum was short so we treasured every moment with her: family times, cuppas, meals, visits to the Doctor, phone calls, everything. Mum coped well but some days were really hard. She was amazing though; she kept her trust in God and said "while there's still life left to live, I'm going to live it"!

A significant day was had only about three weeks before she died when she spent the day with me at our house. We just talked and talked and drank cups of tea! It was during this day together that I remember we were able to be honest and get real about a few things. I faced some of my fears and shared some stuff I'd kept hidden for years out of fear, realising I had nothing to lose and everything to gain. We cleared the air, asked each other for forgiveness, forgave each other, shared some things on a deeper level, came to some further understanding of where we both were at, hugged, cried and laughed.

It was a special mother and daughter day, a day to

get perspective in light of the circumstances and the reality that her time with us was short—a day I look back on with fond memories and am so very grateful we were able to share. It was precious that we had the opportunity to be honest and open and has given me the truth that I have no regrets.

The Rhode to Zimkesalia

19
Anchored in the storm

On 28 September 1995, on a Thursday evening, Mum and Dad popped in for a few minutes to drop something off before they left the next day for Kyabram. It was about 4.30pm and as we stood in the driveway, I begged them to stay for tea. At first they said it was too late and too much trouble but I assured them it wasn't and so they stayed. I don't remember what I made but it was quick and fed us all well. They didn't stay long as Mum was tired and they needed to finish packing. We hugged and said goodbye and I watched their car leave with an ache in my heart and prayers for their safekeeping and for Mum's healing as they drove down the street. I didn't know then, that this was the last day I would see her alive.

The next day, Mum and Dad arrived in Kyabram to visit Shirley and Glenn for a few days on their way to attend a family wedding in Adelaide a week later. Shirley was eight months pregnant with their daughter, Rebecca.

On Saturday night I rang and had a chat with them all and Mum wasn't sounding good at all. When I asked her how she felt, her answer was 'grim'. I told her I loved her and was praying. Dad told me that he would take her to the hospital in the morning if she hadn't improved.

Early Sunday morning she became very ill and

Dad took her to the Kyabram hospital. They managed to make her comfortable again and over the next 36 hours or so, she began to feel a little better and was cheerful and trusting in God, looking forward to the wedding in Adelaide the following week.

On the Tuesday morning, 3 October 1995, Mum died at the age of fifty three. She was whole, healed and home with her beloved Lord.

In spite of our pain, we had to smile at God's sense of humour—He is truly gracious. We used to tease Mum about how much she loved her baths and how much noise she made when she continuously splashed water over herself to keep warm—like a herd of elephants! Well she was in the bath at the Kyabram hospital when Jesus took her home. The nurse had stepped out to get a towel and came back and Mum, relaxed, comfortable and warm, had peacefully slipped away. God cares about the tiniest things.

Dad rang us to let us know Mum had gone and we left Melbourne immediately, taking my brother Jim with us and we had a few days together in Kyabram.

We then all returned and put the wheels in motion for Mum's memorial service a few days later.

From my diary:

10/10/95 Bonnie—Mum—Died 3/10/95—Cremated 9/10/95

I've just lost my Mum. The world seems very black just now—the future too. Somehow, with Your help, Lord, we'll get through this heart wrenching time. Probably, the tears will dry up, but I don't believe the deep ache will ever stop. My mind can't quite comprehend it all—I don't understand. And yet, I know that God is here now—He ministers to the broken hearted—He feels our pain and He IS IN CONTROL! Even when I'm not, He is! Thank you, Lord.

The garden's beautiful— it's spring. I wanted Mum to see it looking so beautiful—and now she won't. But, she's with You, Lord – and your garden's even more beautiful. I suddenly feel closer than ever to her, when I see a beautiful flower, or a view she would have loved. Thank you Lord, for the beautiful day yesterday—the day of Mum's cremation and Thanksgiving Service for her life. It was a cloudless day—blue skies and a gentle breeze. Sun gently touching the earth— Mum would have loved it. She always did love to bask in the sun.

Thank you Lord, for Mum. I realise even more so now, after the service yesterday, how special she was—what an honour and privilege to be her daughter. Lord, let my life be worthy of You, too. Let Your Name be praised and all glory go to You, by the way I live my life each day.

Time is so precious—we're in this world only once—Seize The Day! Help me not to be too tired to care for another—too sad to notice someone else's pain—let this time become a valuable learning and growing time for us all.

And Lord, I want to be the Wife and Mother You want me to be. Mum was so honourable in all her roles—let me be so too. She's a hard act to follow, but then I'm me! Let me take the parts of Mum that I can, and that are relevant, and be a good and patient Mum and serving Wife and Homemaker, as she was. This world has too few people left who really care—let me remember to put others first—as she did. Lord, I then am reminded that she was only the person she was, because of You. She wasn't perfect, but she was Yours! Thank you!

You know, we tend to imagine how we'll cope when bad things happen to us. I'd thought I'd need to be institutionalized when Mum died—I thought I'd never cope.

God is so good though. His strength is made perfect in our weakness. He gives us the grace when we need it, and His grace is sufficient for me. I can't explain the peace and joy that He has given and promised to keep giving, when we just have no one else to turn to. His promise in October 1994 was true. He is Sovereign.

I put down my anchor years ago into the solid rock of Christ and, in spite of the storms and buffeting winds, I am held strong, secure.

20

Miscarriage — the lost opportunity to carry to fruition

In early 1997 I was pregnant again and we began to dream and hope and get all excited—as most couples do as they anticipate the arrival of another child. It was just when I was experiencing the first flutters of movement and we thought we were through the danger period that I had a routine scan and found out that the baby was dead. I was sixteen weeks into the pregnancy. I went to the hospital the following day for a D and C.

I never knew how devastating a miscarriage could be. The waves of pain enveloped me and I could hardly breathe. It felt like a rollercoaster of emotions—shock, anger, deep sadness and wondering why? My body reacted by hemorrhaging and I was made to stay in bed—I was so weak with the loss.

David moved a mattress to the lounge room for me so I could be near my family and I wept buckets of tears—it was not only a loss of our baby but a loss of the dreams, hopes and expectations that we'd had. The other kids would join me on my mattress and just spend time with me as I couldn't believe how fragile and precious life was. We shared many, many hugs through those days.

It gave us opportunities to discuss painful issues of life and death with our young children. We had to help them process their pain, their confusion and together we talked and prayed and read a book we were given (on losing someone near to you) that explained the process of grief, emotions, life, death and heaven.

Our church provided us with meals and we received some beautiful cards and words of comfort from precious people who cared.

Up until now, I hadn't realised the impact and pain that a miscarriage could cause. How we can so often underestimate people's pain and try to explain it away with words we think will help! I spent much time reading my Bible, reading many of the Psalms and finding peace in the Psalmist's agonized prayers to his God from a place of pain. God was my peace and comfort—His word a solace and lifeline. I processed this grief by reading, talking to my family and close friends and allowing God to minister to me. I refused to blame Him as some suggested we do, after all, He is God; our anchor. We named our baby Leigh, not knowing whether this baby was a boy or a girl but somehow we feel he was a boy.

Life, Loss, Love

Life, stirring
Growth, swelling
Hopes and dreams
Plans and imaginings
Mornings of ill
Days of tired
Nights of fluttering movement
And nothing.

Suddenly still,
Plateau
Bewildered faces,
Questions
Something is different
Wrong
Doubts invade,
Fears arise
Imaginations loom large
Tests, doctors

cont.

Serious looks
Sombre moods
Loss of life
Surgery, blood
Tears, confusion
Trust, sadness,
Trust, grief
Hopes died,
Dreams disappear
Horizon looms uncertain
God's presence all around
Trust, comfort,
Peace
Acceptance.
Memories
Sadness
Trust again
Peace
Acceptance.

21

Jesse

By June of that same year, I was pregnant again and all was well. We were so excited but we did have some apprehension. However my doctors assured me there was no need to be concerned and that many people who'd had miscarriages went on to have healthy babies afterwards.

One day in the car, while Dave was driving us down Burwood Highway, I felt compelled to write down a prayer. I looked in the glove box and fished out some paper and wrote: *"Dear God, You—are in control. Your goodness in all I see—You are sovereign. I will tell of Your graciousness and compassion, Your mercy, Your steadfastness, Your faithfulness. Let me not be idle—let me speak and be bold to tell of Your goodness. So much we don't understand, we weep, and fret and worry—YET You are true—You do not forget us—You are still on the throne. Thank you and praise You. Your Word reminds me to "Be still and know that I am God. I am in control"*. The date was 31st October 1997.

Only three weeks later, with only a few (what I'd thought were Braxton Hicks) contractions, I went into labour at 25 weeks and 2 days. It was one of those nights when being very tired, I'd sat on the couch watching the hospital show called RPA—and they were telling the story of a family who'd had a premature baby—all emotional, I'd watched that show and thanked God for my safe pregnancy.

I got up from the couch on my way to go to get ready for bed and realised something was seriously wrong. Suddenly it felt like everything was falling out of me! I called Dave and he immediately rang 000. I lay down on the floor with a pillow under my bottom to allow gravity to keep it all inside and I prayed for my baby. Our other three kids were fast asleep so we called a friend who came and stayed with them while we went to the hospital. I endured a very unpleasant and bumpy ride to Monash Hospital in the ambulance with the paramedics trying their best to stop the contractions, which were coming on very fast. This was late Thursday night, November 20.

We were rushed into a room where I was met by a team of medical people who'd been notified that I was en route. It was all action stations! Questions and more questions and forms to sign—I could tell from the looks on their faces that this was serious.

A strange feeling came over me—I almost felt like I was in a bubble—like I was not actually there myself but looking down on this woman in the delivery room and seeing all the activity happening. It was quite surreal. My emotions were intense and swung from fear and terror, to hope and excitement—praying desperately that our baby would be okay.

They brought in a small bed for David to sleep next to me but we didn't get much sleep. Monitors beeped and someone came in to check on me every little while. I lay there with my heart pounding in my ears and, beginning to feel very strange, I called the nursing staff. I was tingling, felt numbness and my heart was not only racing, it was deafening me! There was some alarm and then I almost went into cardiac arrest from a bad reaction to the Ventolin they'd used to try to stop the contractions. After some hurried discussion, the Ventolin was stopped. There was no choice but to let nature take its course.

They injected me with steroids to try to help the baby's lungs to mature. We also signed a form to be a part of a drug trial where the baby would possibly receive this drug being trialed or a placebo. We grasped at any straw we could and agreed to be a part of it.

During the day on the Friday, our pastor—who was also a close friend—arrived to support us and he and David were in the room with me for hours. The contractions continued and, at 7.51pm on 21 November 1997, our baby boy, Jesse Iain, was born—still completely encased in the membranes of the amniotic bag.

There was an immediate flurry of action as he emerged and was taken to a table where his vital stats were taken and he was put on a ventilator. Within minutes he had sensors on him, intravenous lines into his tiny arm and we were then allowed to see him for a few moments before they took him to the neonatal ward. After a little while I was wheeled through there in a wheelchair and was able to sit next to his incubator and look at him. Words can barely describe the range of emotions I felt that night. I wasn't sure whether to feel happy or devastated. I never did get to hold him close at that time. Not long after, I was taken to my bed and advised to sleep and get my rest while I could.

I could tell over the next few weeks that people didn't know whether to congratulate us or commiserate with us and, to be honest, I didn't know how to feel myself. Overwhelmed didn't even come close. The three weeks following were a whirlwind of emotions: coming and going, loving and caring, crying and laughing, praying and pleading, crying and praying again.

And trusting. Trusting that through it all, God was sovereign and His will would be done. Through it all, our anchor held fast. We so totally believed, and still do, in God's healing power. We know that He works all things together for good for those who love him and we know that He holds our future in His hands.

Romans 8:28 (NIV) *"And we know that in all things God works for the good of those who love Him, who have been called according to His purpose."*

Excerpts from my diary: Sat. 22 November 1997

'What a tiny baby! Can hardly believe my eyes. Only 769g weight (1.7lbs) and 32.5cm long. So small. Breathing with ventilator—intravenous lines into his arm, umbilical cord, sensors on his chest, tummy and foot. Tube in his nose to lungs. Wow! Very scary to see and so small. Almost transparent skin. They say first seventy-two hours most critical. Romans 8:28—all. Now it's watch, wait, pray. ...Spent time together or 'in shifts' watching and talking to Jesse and praying with him. Susanne & Melville brought Michael, Megan and Sarah in to us—so special to see them too. Took photos—spent time with kids—talked— tried to explain things.'

Sun. am 23 November

'Awoke to Janna (Neonatal Dr) knocking at my door before 6am. She said Jesse had a pulmonary hemorrhage during night—hopefully will live through next couple of hours—basically it was bleeding in lungs, which may have caused bleeding in brain too. They had to use drugs ...to keep him calm. She said to call Dave and come see him, but not to be too shocked, as he was very still and very pale. Also very bruised. Oh Lord, why, what, how? NO, God is still in control. He is able to do ANYTHING! I still believe this is our Miracle Baby! Reading Your Word —Psalms—many of them—

tears, many of them... Thank you for all these promises, Lord. I claim them for Jesse, for us and I know, ultimately, You're in control! Rom. 8:28

...but Lord, no matter how you choose to use this situation, may we know You know best and that our lives—all our lives—are in His hands. Thank you Lord...I pray that Jesse's life and ours, may be witnesses to all around us and that all glory will go to you, Lord. Use us Lord, help us to be willing..Gee, I miss Mum. Mum, I can even picture you 'clucking' over Jesse at his crib side— checking all the dials and switches, all the drugs, all the sensors and I can, most of all, imagine you praying for him. What a precious picture. All the while turning to hug me and reassure me too. And if this is how a precious Mum would be, how much more so, a God in control!!!'

Sat 29 November

'Wow, a week has passed! Today Jesse is eight days old! (26wks 3d gestation). God is working. What a week! Monday was a tough day. They did a brain ultrasound and discovered extensive bleeding. Dr A R, the consultant, came to talk with us—he believes it's so bad we should not continue supporting Jesse. Inevitable brain damage affecting both sides of brain—motor control and intellect. I've never received worse news in my life. We sat there, stunned... Basically, according to medical opinion, Jesse's life is less worth living if brain damaged than not and so we should avoid that. Chances are he may not live anyway. What kind of decision is that?! We will not give up. Praying for the Lord's will in this. Please don't ask us to make such a decision. If Jesse is to live, let him live, if not, please Lord, you take him...Second scan showed no change. Still trusting that God will heal Jesse in His timing. One nurse said she sensed peace and blessing over Jesse and that corner of the room (Bay 7). When Louise and Lawrence were in, we all knelt and prayed together in my room. Later that day the nurse in charge came in and said she was a Christian too—and could sense my room was full of the Holy Spirit —she said it gave her goose bumps! Wow Lord, You're already using this situation *for Your glory—thank you. Continue to use us and Jesse—keep us obedient and faithful to You, as You are ever faithful to us. Thank You for Your Peace. All the while, I'm expressing milk—Jesse taking 1ml per 4 hours since Thurs/Fri—a little stop/starting as his gut gets used to it. Fed through tube in nose to tummy. Poor little chap.'*

On Thursday night, December 11, Dave and I had spent the evening with Jesse until after midnight, when we needed to go home and get some rest. We talked all the way home, discussing whether we would agree to a procedure the medical staff were recommending we have done on Jesse early the next morning. It was a procedure to insert a tube into the brain, which could be easily used to drain excess fluid off the brain to stop brain swelling. We stopped off at the supermarket on the way home to get milk and bread and decided the decision could be made when we awoke the next morning. We fell into bed exhausted at just after 1.30am.

As soon as our heads hit the pillows, we got a phone call. The hospital told us we'd better get back there soon as Jesse had taken a turn for the worse. Adrenalin kicked in and we raced back as fast as we could. Running up the stairs into the neonatal unit, we stopped short when we saw Jesse's bed surrounded by staff and approached apprehensively.

Straight away, we knew we were too late. On December 12, 1997, in the neonatal ward at the Monash NICU (Neonatal Intensive Care Unit), our precious baby Jesse went to be with Jesus. He had died only moments before, while we would have been parking the car, and they were beginning to remove the tubes and intravenous lines from his body. One of the staff who had been amazingly supportive to us, wrapped him up and put him in my arms. This was my first proper hold. He was still warm, but lifeless. We were steered into a little room where we sat down holding our baby boy and just stared at him stunned.

I looked at David's face and couldn't believe how closed off he looked—the pain was deeply etched into every part of his gentle self and yet I could see he was trying so hard to be strong for me. I felt numb. Could this really be happening? Could the intensity of the past three weeks be over? Was this little baby going to be only a memory? I sat there unable to believe the reality of this moment. I stroked his little face, now beginning to cool, and the horror of his death choked me to the core. I sat there willing him to take a breath, to open his eyes, desperately begging God to raise him from the dead, not quite able to absorb the reality of the moment.

I needed to speak to someone—to Mum, but she wasn't there; why wasn't Mum there when I needed her? Why was she also dead? The pain made my mind erratic with random thoughts and I had to consciously remember my anchor— my God, my Rock, my stabilizer in the storm.

Dad was overseas and I didn't care about the time difference. We rang him and told him the news. He was very quiet and serious on the phone and told me he loved me, which made me cry even more. It was so precious to hear that from him. And knowing he was my Dad, I knew that he would be hurting for us and it pained me to make it so but I needed him to know.

I then rang my sister Shirley and told her that Jesse was gone. I happened to ring just when she was sitting on the side of her bed, in labour with her third child, about to leave for the hospital. Oh how awful I felt that she was in labour about to give birth to her baby—a day that should have been full of joy and I was dampening her day with my sad news. She had her baby boy, Ryan, about three hours after Jesse went to be with the Lord, on 12 December 1997. A bitter sweet day.

Our pastor, who had been closely connected with us over those weeks, arrived and sat quietly with us. He prayed with us, let us talk, cry and process out loud. His patience and love was immeasurable and meant so much to us.

We rang home and I spoke to my brother Jim, who was with our other kids and told him the news. He was understandably quiet and saddened for us. We asked him not to tell the kids but to get them ready and we'd be home soon to pick them up. We got home and told them the news. This was hard as they hadn't been as intensely involved as us. We had tried to keep routine as normal as possible for them over the previous weeks, even though it had been difficult. Their reactions ranged from sadness and tears to lots of questions and a quiet uncertainty.

We returned to the hospital with our other children and spent a couple of hours with Jesse's body, allowing each one of the kids to say their goodbyes to their brother and to understand he was really gone. As time went by, his body became blue-ish which was hard to explain to an almost three-year-old who had multiple matter-of-fact questions. Each one of our children processed their grief differently and we tried to let each one know that their way of grieving was okay; we're all different, so it's good to process it as we each must. We huddled together in our grief and cried together and we prayed together. It was very important to me to let our kids see our faith in action, that hope was not lost, that God was still in control and still on His heavenly throne in spite of our loss. We kissed our baby boy goodbye and went home without him.

Never, never, never have we felt that kind of pain. It's indescribable. It seemed our hearts were screaming out in pain—we could hardly breathe. I remember Dave and me lying on our bed in tears, holding each other close and he expressing a wish to sleep till the pain went away. It broke my heart but endeared him to me further. He's so tough on the outside but so soft inside.

Through this rollercoaster of emotions, there were the odd crazy snippets of thought that threatened to cast doubt and raise anger at God but instantly, with complete conviction, we knew they were not of God. We knew that God is in control and His plans are best. We trust that He holds us in His big, loving hands and that we are part of a plan that perhaps we don't yet understand but is what is best and right. Never have we felt so close to God, either. Never have we had such peace and confidence in our Almighty God. His thoughts are not our thoughts, nor are His ways our ways.

He comforts, He holds us close, He is God.

Jeremiah 29:11 (NIV) *"For I know the plans I have for you," declares the Lord, "plans to prosper you and not to harm you, plans to give you hope and a future."*

Isaiah 55:8,9 (NIV) *"For My thoughts are not your thoughts, neither are your ways My ways," declares the Lord. "As the heavens are higher than the earth, so are My ways higher than your ways and My thoughts than your thoughts."*

Lamentations 3:21-23 (NIV) *"Yet this I call to mind and therefore I have hope: Because of the Lord's great love we are not consumed, for His compassions never fail. They are new every morning; great is Your faithfulness."*

Our precious boy went to be with God but his frail,

little body still had to be buried and we chose to bury him in the Children's Lawn Graves section at Lilydale Memorial Park. It was a lovely day and etched in my memory is the picture of my darling man carrying his son in a tiny little white coffin and laying it in place, ready for burial. Our dearest friends and family stood around as we farewelled our baby boy—till we meet again, Jesse. It's a beautiful place with undulating green fields all around, trees, flowers—an air of serenity and peace.

David wrote this prayer and he read it out at Jesse's service:

> Lord Jesus,
> Today as we remember our tiny baby boy,
> Jesse Iain, we come with sadness
> and yet with hearts of thanksgiving.
> We have been so privileged to know
> and love Jesse for three weeks.
> A gift of God. Thank you.
> This baby boy, so small, so perfect to see,
> with tiny fingers and toes,
> his beautiful eyes and
> soft little mouth, all of him,
> has impacted on so many lives
> in so short a space of time.
> Lord, we asked for Your will to be done.
> We believed You could do a miracle and You have.
>
> Jesse has touched so many.
> We've learnt so much and now
> You hold him close to Your heart.
> He is healed and whole – complete in You.
> Thank you. We love You Lord.
> Amen.

This beautiful prayer moved my heart so much. It came from a place deep within David's heart. A man of few words, who feels deeply and expressed his love for God and Jesse in this simple prayer. I love him all the more.

A tough day: I sensed our closest friends and family's sadness as they supported us that day, some of whom had very little idea of what to say. Just their presence with us meant so much; no-one could really say a thing. I could see my brother Jim struggling with it all and it was tough to see him trying to process it. More about Jim a bit later. It was a desperately sad day but not without hope.

It was a full day. In the morning we buried our son Jesse and in the evening, our son Michael had his Grade 6 graduation ceremony and celebration dinner from primary school. What a day of extreme emotions, we were so very proud of our eldest son who shone as he received awards for his achievements that night. But it also made us conscious of the fact that we'd never do that with Jesse.

Over time, our little Jesse boy has never left our memory. His short life was not in vain. As a couple and as a family, we learnt so much during that painful time but we have also learnt that we can survive and not only survive, but thrive. We have come through this experience and we still have strong faith in God. He is able to get us through whatever we go through. We have chosen repeatedly to put our trust in the anchor we have put down into the seas of life and God is our rock.

Over the years, we have visited Jesse's grave in Lilydale and, many a time, I have just gone there for a few minutes of peace and quiet and to contemplate all that God has done since Jesse's short life impacted ours so greatly.

God's Word talks about telling the story, of His greatness and faithfulness through it all, as a testimony of His truth, comfort and love and that is why I write this.

22

Dad meets Rosa

In the meantime, Dad had returned to South Africa for a couple of years to work with World Vision and whilst there, he met a lady called Rosa.

When Jesse died, Dad surprised us and came back for his funeral and supported us through those tough days. It was very special to answer the doorbell and find him standing there. Tears flowed.

The night before he left, Dad told us, quite shyly almost, that he had met someone and was rather keen on her! We of course were thrilled but at the same time we were nervous too. What would this lady be like? Would she accept us? Would she change Dad? It wasn't long after he returned to South Africa that we received a phone call in January to say that they were engaged and planning to marry in March.

We quickly went into frantic mode trying to figure out a way to travel back for their wedding, which we did manage to do, refinancing our home.

Two days before the wedding we arrived and met Rosa. She and Dad came to visit us at David's Mum's home where we were staying. She walked in and, I don't know what I'd expected, she was lovely. She was a woman of grace and poise and even though she must have been nervous to meet us too, she didn't show it. During the course of the evening, she told me that she knew she wasn't Mum and knew she could never take Mum's place and we were free to speak of Mum as often as we wanted to, and not to feel we couldn't as she was clearly a large part of our lives. I was so blessed by her statement and it felt good that she didn't feel threatened by Mum. The reality is, Mum's shoes are way too big for anyone to ever fill.

Two days later, Dad and Rosa married in March 1998, with a beautiful, simple and Godly wedding.

This was another new and huge family adjustment. God is so good. Dad is so blessed to have been married to a woman like my Mum, and then to be given another woman so amazingly lovely and special like Rosa. She has never once tried to take Mum's place and her sensitivity to us and our grief was special. We love her and she is a part of our family. We often laugh as they are so amusingly and perfectly matched! I thank God for her and that Dad has her in his life.

Whilst in South Africa, we enjoyed a seven-week holiday, caught up with old friends and family and did a few tourist things. We enjoyed being back on the continent of Africa and showing our older children where they'd been born and a little of their background before we moved to Australia.

One of our memories of this trip was struggling to get Sarah—who was only just three—to take malaria tablets. We all needed to take anti-malarials, since we visited malaria infested areas whilst seeing some wildlife. It was like World War III trying to get them into her, until a different pharmacist told us we could use an alternative medication, which was more palatable. Oh what a relief!

Below I am including an excerpt from my journal written on another visit back to South Africa in August

2007.
Schotia Private Game Reserve, at dusk

Oh, words fail to describe the sense of awe that you feel as you sit in silence and watch the most incredible, awe inspiring sunset you've ever seen in your life. The bush sounds just continue on—the odd bird cries out, small creatures scuttle away in the grass, the insects buzz —and there is a sense of insignificance as you sit there and realise the awesomeness of God and the amazing beauty He is able to create, the emotions it evokes, the smells of the bush, the clean air, the distant roar of the lions, the cry of the eagle.

The colours are almost hard to believe—the shades of blue to indigo, to orange and red and yellow and purple, all spread out across the endless sky. The world takes on a crimson glow, an eeriness stalks the atmosphere. The sun sinks fast below the horizon, leaving a stillness fraught with the expectation of danger lurking in the shadows. Some creatures are settling in for the night and others are just beginning their nocturnal hunt, the wildlife continues in its natural instinct to survive the harsh conditions of the African bush.

We sat in silence atop the game viewing truck and drank in the splendour of the experience. Slowly, the voices began to whisper, mingled with the click of camera shutters trying in vain to capture the essence of such raw beauty.

I didn't want to leave—I could have sat there forever, if only for the fact that the sun was gone and our tummies were beginning to rumble with hunger! We drove on and suddenly we stopped.

There, as we rounded a corner and in the light of our truck were five lions. A male, two females and two cubs, not too new, probably teenagers. They were just beginning to awake, and yawned lazily, as they stretched and looked annoyed at the lights being shone at them. The large male got up and playfully rolled one of the females over and they stood up, looking at us. This was a rather frightening experience. My eight-year-old son spoke and the females' eyes fixed on him as though he would be easy prey. We didn't stay long. They were getting ready to hunt and we drove away reluctantly.

23
My dear brother Jim

Over the months before Jesse was born, my brother Jim had been living with us. He had studied Outdoor Education at Bendigo and had made friends with a group of people who were passionately environmentally conscious. He was a young man who loved God with passion but became increasingly frustrated at the world around him, with so many Christians living complacently, so much inequality, so much greed and hypocrisy. In many ways, he was an idealist: gentle, caring, a lover of the unlovely.

While Jim was living with us, it became clear that he was suffering from depression. We discovered he was smoking marijuana and had been for some time. It was a catalyst of horrific change. It altered his mind and he became so confused. His mind played tricks on him and life became hell. He was diagnosed with paranoid schizophrenia but objected to using medication.

Having him live with us was a rollercoaster adventure-cum-nightmare. It was great at times but awful at others. We had long philosophical debates and he was exhausting. David really struggled with him, having been in law enforcement in years gone by and now having to deal with a brother-in-law who hated authority. It was a real challenge for him. I often felt as though I was stuck in the middle, I loved them both, but could also understand their differing opinions.

At heart and when he was doing well, Jim was mischievous and such fun. He could take off many accents and having lived in Kenya, had the African, Indian and Arab accents down pat! He also loved great music—some quite alternative. One song that always reminds me of him is 'Wild Thing' by the Troggs.

He was a great cook and loved spicy food. One day he cooked us curry and we could barely eat it, while he added extra chilli to his plate and sat there enjoying it and dripping with sweat as he savoured every mouthful, grinning mischievously! I think he enjoyed our reaction to him eating it too! He also taught me to make dahl.

I remember walking into the kitchen one day and he didn't see me come in from behind. I noticed he was eating Milo out of the tin and so I said 'boo!'—well he got such a fright and sprayed Milo everywhere as he choked on it through his laughter—it was hilarious and a special memory I have of him.

His behaviour ranged from fun loving and peaceful to raging anger and threatening violence—and everything in between.

Thankfully things were peaceful and amiable when Jim left. It was a rainy day and he packed his backpack and gave me a kiss and a hug and walked out of the front door and down the road—I watched him go with a heavy heart, never realising he was leaving forever.

He travelled North to Queensland and stayed with Shirley and Glenn briefly. That wasn't easy for them either. Then he left there and headed north again.

Unfortunately, his illness caused Jim to act completely out of character and there was some damage to property, which meant he was arrested. My sister and I were in contact with the authorities and in spite of feeling in some ways that we risked hurting his feelings, we felt the need to have Jim hospitalized for his own safety. After a while, he was sent to a psychiatric hospital for about three months.

He was doing well on medication and I began to feel he was in a good place and starting to return to the Jim we knew. The phone calls were more frequent and so precious. If I ever said 'I love you Jim', he always answered, 'same same'. On the last call I had with him, I said 'I love you Jim', and he said 'I love you too, Cath'. I will always treasure that. After about three months in this hospital, Jim was allowed to go out for a few weeks to stay with Shirley and Glenn.

He'd been out of hospital a week, when he didn't come home one night. He took his own life by hanging on the 20 September 1998.

My legs didn't hold me up when two police officers came to the door and told us the news—I just sunk onto the chair that was quickly pulled out for me. I'd known something was wrong the whole day; one friend described me as having 'ants in my pants' all day!

Shirl had let me know by phone around lunchtime that Jim hadn't come home but we didn't know where he was at that stage and I'd said to her to call the police and let them know, since he was staying at her place. All day I'd been restless and in the late afternoon I'd gone for an early shower, wanting to just lie on the couch and be warm and cozy, when the police arrived.

Why? How? No more, God! I can't take anymore, God!!!! It all seemed too much. Again our hearts cried out in pain—so much pain. It was a suffocating, excruciating pain, a despair that threatened to swallow us whole. It couldn't be, could it? Disbelief and anger rose and waned, along with a myriad of wild emotions.

Where do you turn? How does one process this kind of news? What could I do to make it go away? So many regrets—could I have done something different; could we have prevented this? Who could I blame? How could I fix this? It's not natural; it shouldn't be. It must be able to be fixed. Turn the clock back and change something! I wished it was a nightmare I could wake from but, no, this nightmare was real! Nothing could be done.

We had only one choice. Our anchor. Our hope. Our loving God. How do people do this life without Him in their lives? How do people process this grief without a pinprick of hope at the end of the dark tunnel? We can't possibly know! Still, we asked why?

But you know, God is a God of love and compassion and He has held us all over the years—why not now? And so He did. He does. He still is and always will. What a privilege we have in knowing God and that He is so completely in control of our lives if we let Him have the reins. He is my confidence, my anchor. *"See, I have engraved you on the palms of my hands..."* Isaiah 49:16a (NIV)

However, we're not perfect. There have been many times when we've faltered and been angry at the situations and questioned all He's allowed to happen to us but, ultimately, we're His children and He knows what's best for us. We need to surrender and trust Him as He told me to do so many years ago. He knows the future and won't give us a river to cross without a bridge or miraculously parting the waters and making a way through where there has seemed to be no way. Again, I have had to remember to view life through His filters and not my own.

Jim's funeral was amazing. There were lots of young

people there who loved him and were in so much shock. Jim's death caused a lot of them to really think more deeply about their purpose and why they're here. A passionate group of idealists who, we pray, in God's time, will come to know Jesus out of their own pain and use their passion for His Kingdom.

One of Jim's special friends who we only met after Jim died, has become a friend to us, although we had spoken on the phone before then. She is a beautiful person who is living her life for God and I know that her life was impacted by Jim's life and his influence had something to do with who she has become and the lives she now impacts in her walk with God. This is very precious to my heart.

A week after Jim's death, I sat at the piano and sang what came from my heart. I can't find the words I wrote but the gist was that I would praise Him in the midst of it all and give God the glory, for He is my help. I've learnt that the key to breakthrough is thanksgiving. When we choose to praise out of pain, the peace comes. How awesome is that kind of God!

"Because You are my help, I sing in the shadow of Your wings. My soul clings to You; Your right hand upholds me." Psalm 63:7,8 (NIV)

The Rhode to Zimkesalia

24

Hope rises with new life

Only about a week or so after Jim's death, I became pregnant again. I felt it was like God said there would be joy again, in spite of the pain. This was a tough pregnancy. Given what we'd been through in recent years, there was much apprehension and caution. Since I had been diagnosed with cervical incompetence, which is why I gave birth to Jesse so early, I had to have a cervical stitch put in and I had to stay in bed, lying on my back, allowing gravity to work for almost five months of this pregnancy.

As you could probably imagine, this wasn't easy with three active kids at home! We had some great support from friends and family, the kids were taken and brought home from school and kinder and we had a steady supply of meals given to us from people in and out of the church. One lovely lady came every week to clean the house.

Our bedroom became a bit like a family room, where the kids would come and sit to chat to me after their days at school. I spent many hours with Sarah on the bed with me, playing with Lego, dressing Barbie dolls, reading stories, doing drawings and other creative artworks, which she loved, and basically keeping each other company.

Mentally this was a challenging few months. I remember feeling so lazy, until a friend reminded me that my body was working hard to grow and produce a healthy baby so it was okay for me just to relax. Spiritually, in spite of imminent and hovering depression, I had no choice but to cling to God, to hope, to trust and to rely on Him through it all.

The pregnancy progressed well however, in spite of the risks, and at 36 weeks I had the cervical stitch removed, fully expecting to go into labour which the doctor had told me to be prepared for! Well I didn't! I began to get up a bit more and walk around and slowly but surely, became a little more active! It was so good to be up and vertical after so long flat on my back!

The frustrating part was that mentally, I had been expecting my baby to be early again and, when the 40th week rolled around, I felt quite ripped off! I wasn't sleeping; I was over it big time!

So, at 40 weeks and 2 days, in June 1999, I was induced and our baby Joshua was born. Now he's a miracle! God certainly protected that pregnancy! What a blessing to have Josh after so much pain and sadness. A delightful joy and such a boy!

We have been so blessed with our children. Michael, Megan, Sarah and Joshua are such wonderful, amazing kids. Yeah, I know we're biased, but they really are.

25
Family reflections

Our lives have not been easy—our marriage hasn't been all rosy. I have had to deal with eliminating the baggage that I carried into our marriage from past relationships. Through prayer I have spiritually cut off the unhealthy soul ties[1] and had to obey God in practical ways like throwing away photos and reminders of my past relationships and choosing to forgive those who caused me pain and hurt.

I've had to recognise that my husband is my life partner, companion and head of our home. He is not my God. It was quite a revelation one day, when I realised I was expecting David to be my lover, my comforter, my counselor, my advisor, my security, my provider, my friend, my confidante, my be all and end all and everything in between! He was never designed to fulfill every one of my needs and yet I was expecting him to. Our friendship and marriage began to flourish when I gave him the space to be who he was meant to be and not everything else I needed as well.

Neither has parenting and the raising of our children been easy. We have made mistakes, many that I am sure have long lasting effects but always we bring

---

[1]. Soul ties are a spiritual connection between two people who have been physically intimate with each other or who have had an intense emotional or spiritual association or relationship.

it back to align it with the Word of God, and His unit of measurement, to see how we should be doing life as a family. My prayers are that God will fill the gaps we left and bring healing and restoration to the damage we may have caused our kids and that each of our children, in their own right and at their own time, will come to understand that we did try to do the right thing, as my parents did too, and that there can be forgiveness and moving on from there.

Throughout this life journey of mine has been the everyday stuff that just happens: the sleepless nights, the feeds, the nappy changes, the vomits, the tickles, the laughter, tripping over toys on the floor, mounds of washing, peanut butter kisses and sticky fingers, good night stories and prayers, unmade beds and wet towels, school projects, concerts, graduations, sports training and sports games, dance lessons, music lessons, missed buses and forgotten lunches, injuries, hospital visits, appendicitis, tonsillitis, stitches and bruises, the teaching, training, the praying and the listening.

We've helped our kids navigate through their friendship issues, prayed frantic prayers asking God to remove certain unhealthy friendships, and have had prayers answered when good friends have stepped in. Their fears, their hopes, their dreams, the chats, the arguments, the fights, the tears, the rebellion, the making up, the hugs, the love, the forgiveness, the joys, the parties, the celebrations, the fun, the laughter, the 'Dad' jokes, the wit, the puns and the sillyness, the pets, new clothes, the cleaning of rooms, the holidays, the memories—so many life experiences as a family.

Parenting our kids through their teens is a challenge we are still in the process of dealing with. Each of our children has been so unique that the method that worked for one didn't necessarily work for the others. We have found that being super open and honest with our kids is our preferred way of parenting. As a young person, I found there was so much secrecy that I didn't feel trusted and I believe it only served to feed my sense of insecurity. We have chosen to be a lot more open with our children in the hope and trust that God will give them a measure of maturity to handle what we choose to share with them. Of course, there is still a sense of confidentiality within this openness, for which we have had to pray for wisdom.

I've had to face my 'stuff' along the way as I've raised my kids too. One day when Michael was about fourteen, he came and asked me how long pregnancy was. When I told him it was usually about nine months, he argued with me and said that it couldn't be as he was born only six months after we got married. I looked directly at him and said "yes, you were, and yes, pregnancy is nine months long". You could see the cogs turning in his head as he processed that bit of information and slowly the truth dawned on him. He was so shocked and just said, "Mum! Seriously? Not you and Dad, Mum?" I just said, "yes Mike, Dad and I did the wrong thing". I then explained to him that we didn't start off ideally but he was truly wanted and loved and definitely NO mistake! God in His grace had forgiven us and grown us into wholeness through Him and blessed our marriage and family.

This conversation revealed to me at that stage that at least Mike was shocked and found it hard to get his head around this. It indicated that our lives and witness had changed enough for him to notice it, even as our son.

Sometimes we have had to pray God's protection

over our kids as we have tried not to parent out of our own inadequacies and fear. There have been many times we have had to trust that God has it all in control. I have literally paced the floor in our home and in my bedroom with my Bible in my hands and spoken out loud to the enemy, telling him to keep his hands off my kids and declaring God's promises over them again and again.

God's Word says that we don't fight against flesh and blood but against principalities and powers and I have had to stand my ground in spiritual warfare and take authority over the enemy and the evil he wishes to bring into our family's lives.

The power of the spoken Word of God is something we may not quite fathom but it's the Word of Almighty God so I have declared His Words over situations and still do and, even when we haven't seen results, we still trust that His power is at work.

Prayer is a powerful tool and so is thanksgiving. These weapons are my choice when I am interceding for my family. God has shown me how precious His Word is and how powerful these tools are that He has made available to us if we will only use them! I will always keep praying for our family; I will never back down and never give up. This now extends not only to my own children but also their partners and their children too. I claim the scriptures that talk of God's blessing that extends to the next generations and the next and I know He hears my prayers. I trust His promises.

As our older two have left home and married, there has been the tension of having to let go and yet still a holding on to our wider family unit and valuing the preciousness in that. There is clearly a sense of loss that I have felt as a mother, as I've had to navigate the letting go and letting be and trusting them entirely into God's hands. And this part isn't over, we have two others who, in time, will leave home and become independent as well.

Being a very visual person, I like to see the family ties as being a little like bungee cords, flexible and stretchy, not to be entirely cut off—merely flexible enough to stretch away allowing independence and growth but still connected in the wider family sense, like a network or web that evolves and flexes with life's surging growth and expansion. Flexibility in families builds unity and there is strength in numbers.

In a broken society, I so often just praise God for our family, for the love we all share, the fun and the laughter and everything that makes life just so precious! I believe our choice at the start of our marriage to make it work, to keep Christ central in our marriage and family, is key to our survival. God is able to make perfect what began as imperfect and even though we're a long way from perfect now, He is working in and through us and continuing to grow us closer to Him and to one another as we remain anchored to Him.

I look back to my upbringing and often think of a verse I know my parents believed and hung onto for us: Proverbs 22:6 (KJV) *Train up a child in the way he should go, And when he is old he will not depart from it.*

That training I believe, is what sank that anchor deep into the rock that is our God, the One who is immovable. Even when storms toss us all about, He holds us strong.

We, to the best of our human ability and with the help and grace of God, have tried to do this with our children too. I believe we see frequent rewards of that in each of them now, as each one navigates their own lives.

In spite of our humble beginnings, God has been so

good to us. It's a full life with so much to be thankful for. Again, and again, we praise God for His faithfulness to us and for His rich blessings!

I am truly and absolutely grateful to both my parents and my grandparents for the Christian heritage and the legacy I have been given. I plan to also leave those for my children and their children too. It is a generational blessing.

I am also truly thankful for the heritage David had. There is a wealth of Godliness and wisdom surrounding him too.

26

Mom's visits

We were so excited and blessed to have David's Mom come and stay for about seven weeks in late 2000. We had been so devastated when we heard that she'd had breast cancer, then surgery and was undergoing chemotherapy. The hardest part was being so far away. Living on a different continent to our family in Africa makes the distance seem more pronounced when there's illness.

So it was wonderful when Mom decided to visit and we caught up and shared much through that time. She recovered well from her treatment, Joshua got to meet his Grandmother and the other kids were able to reconnect.

In autumn 2004, Dave's Mom spent another eight weeks with us in Melbourne. Although we were busy, we had an awesome time together, chatting, laughing, reconnecting, sharing more deeply on a spiritual level and just appreciating time together again and being family.

She visited again in 2010 when our daughter Meg got married and again with David's sister Gill, when Meg's first baby Jessie was three months old in 2011. They were very precious times and extra special for Mom to see her first Great Grandchild too.

In all her trips we've done a little sightseeing but

the most valued times spent together have been those long chats and cuppas, as she has found that is what she enjoys best and we just love having her doing life with us here too. We so love and miss her and wish the trips could be more frequent.

27
Keeping the faith — let's get practical

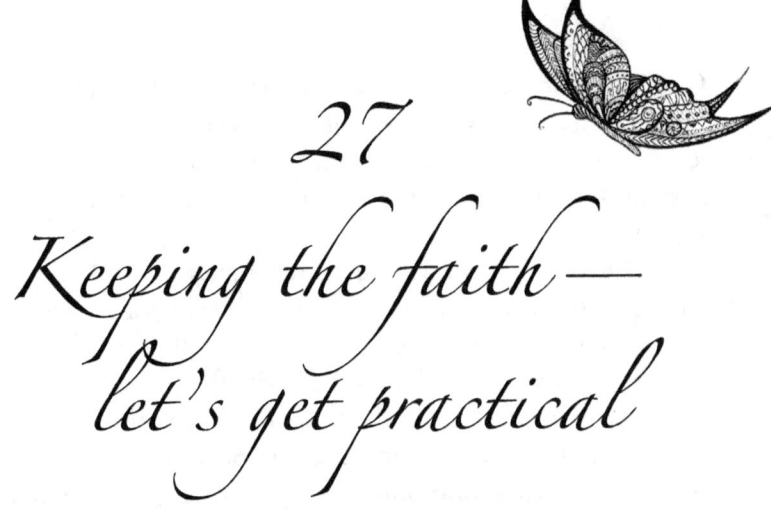

Someone asked me how I keep my faith amidst all I've gone through in my life. Honestly, my question is rather, 'how do I not keep it?' The alternative is something that I don't care to think about. It's not an option. It's without HOPE and I need hope to live. I'm all about HOPE! I hang onto my faith with every fibre of my being and am thankful that in all my hanging on, He holds me. Tight!

How does someone like me describe and give a practical idea of how I connect with God and spend my time with Him? Well, I really don't have a set routine. I'm a bit random. My mother used to say that the first thing we should read each day should be our Bible. What we think about most or first, is our 'God' or our 'idol'.

And having grown up in a strong Bible teaching church environment, I can be inclined to be rather 'religious' and have a 'religious' view of how to do things. But I don't want to be religious. I don't want rules and legalism to drive and fuel me.

I want to WANT to read because I desire it. I want to find out more about Him because I desire to know my

God— to know the one I love, who loves me too. There are times it feels easy because it's easy when you're in love, other times it's out of commitment but it's what is right. I learnt years ago that it is 'right to do, what it is right to do'.

Of course, and with all of this in my mind, I've struggled to make my times with God a thing of the heart without all the religious 'oughts' that go with it; without the guilt attached and the legalistic ritual.

Why do I even WANT to spend time with God? Because as I get to know my Creator, Saviour and the One who has the truest and purest perspective, I get to catch a little of His perspective too.

Instead of viewing 'religion', the 'Bible' or 'faith' through the world's filter or lens, I get to view the world through God's eyes—His perspective of the world, life, circumstances, everything—through the filter or lens of His Truth, His Word and His mind. Why wouldn't I want to? I need to! And I'm human so sometimes the image I see is still distorted, even if slightly, but that is why I need His Word.

So here is what I do and it's changed over time and continues to change with the season I'm in. I guess it starts with the fact that I know God's Word is Truth and I believe it. This conviction has been with me most of my life and I believe it is what I have referred to as my anchor. I am held fast to my God, the One I'm connected to, who is immovable and strong. God is faithful—He is there; He is consistent; He loves me. Viewing life through His filter or lens is the only way to thrive, flourish and live fully!

Another key is being filled with the Holy Spirit. Allowing Him to interpret God's Word and speak to me is vital. He makes it relevant, gives me revelation, shows me

God's perspective and reveals Truth.

So I read my Bible—a section of it most days — sometimes it is just a verse, sometimes chapters, sometimes more, sometimes less. I pray before I start and I ask the Holy Spirit to show me something specific—sometimes a verse or even just a word jumps out at me, sometimes nothing! However I know this—the Word of God is ALIVE, it is POWERFUL and it has AUTHORITY—so if I get it into me, I am equipping myself with weaponry which will come in handy if needed. Maybe I will need it now, maybe later. So I discipline myself to read it, whether I feel like it or not.

I go through seasons of reading devotionals and journaling too, which I've found are hugely beneficial as well. These days, I journal more than I used to. I think this is because I understand the value it is to me and it gives me something I can go back to, to remind myself what God's been saying to me.

Some days life is so busy I don't get the time to sit down for long but I can still get the Word into my heart and spirit through other means.

I believe in this day and age as we have access to so much technology that we can have the Word in our hearts and minds and ears all day if we choose to. I listen on my phone apps, on my laptop, in my car, as I do housework. We have so many resources at our fingertips that it isn't hard to be in the zone—no matter what we're doing—if we choose to. And to be honest, sometimes I zone out too—and a chapter later I realise I haven't been listening, but my spirit's heard it and the very next verse I might notice is just what I needed that day.

Of course, it's important to make those times of solitude and silence with God a priority. He speaks into attuned and listening ears more easily than if we're on the run.

There have been seasons in my life when a set time has worked for me, to sit quietly with my Bible, a cup of tea and a notebook and pen. Other times it hasn't. I don't think God is expecting anything specific of us, we are all different and in different seasons of life. He wants us to be in communion with Him no matter what, so make it work for you. He understands.

Another precious part of my time with God is music. Being a lover of music ever since I can remember and as an act of love towards my God, I love to worship and praise Him and using music makes it so easy!

I love to sing or listen to worship music, sometimes quiet and contemplative and sometimes loud so I get up and dance around. I do this even when alone, as I love to enjoy the way God has created us to enjoy and celebrate Him through music.

I make playlists of selected songs which encourage and build me up during tough times. I have found listening to certain songs on repeat almost drills truth into my heart when my life is so hard that my faith feels dry and needs building up.

Many times I sit at the piano or pick up my guitar and just play whatever is on my heart. He speaks to me through music whether I'm listening to it or writing my own. I have enjoyed and continue to enjoy many intimate moments with the Composer of Life's Song.

I believe that even though my times with God have not been as consistent as I'd ideally have liked, He has met me, spoken with me, comforted me, been my strength and is my Father, my Friend, my anchor and my constant companion through every day.

It is because He is always there, always consistent and always faithful, that I have kept my faith strong—not because of anything I have done or can do. He is the Faithful One.

My God is always good, no matter what; my circumstances or life situations don't change that. We live in a fallen world. We share in the suffering of Christ.

Thankfully Still

The whole of life can be a race
A rush from thing to thing
But if we stop and change our pace
Take time to think
Slow our minds, slow our hearts,
Embrace the grace
We learn it has a timeless ring
This a precious thing
An essence so profound, so real, that raw
And pain can turn with mercy
Into something true and whole, felt
Moments of wonder and beauty,
pure with clarity
Emerge from what was destined not to be so
Miracles to hold, to cherish, to grow
Gratitude born of adversity,
thankfulness raised
A heart closed tight opens —
petals in the sunlight
It drinks in all of God's promise
Beautiful.
Time.
Still.

His Love

*Gentleness, grace,
Mercy like a river, flows
Saturating sin and cleansing
The stubborn stain on heart
Confession, surrender
Forgiveness, made new
His blood washes clean
White, white as snow
This is love.*

Harmony of Love

Lover of my Soul
Composer of Life's Song
He writes and creates
Every note it vibrates
With Joy, with Hope
With Love's amazing song
He sings to me
And I sing to Him
Together we combine
A Harmony of Love.

The blend of notes
The mountain peaks
The valleys deep
The smooth plateaus
Each one alone
Would be too much
But together they blend
Make a beautiful sound
The colours of life
A Harmony of Love.

He Dances with Me

Broken, I kneel at Your feet
My heart is wrenching
Weeping, I'm filled with regret
Lord, I repent, Lord I repent
The tears run down my face
Falling, in awe of Your grace.

Gentle hands lift me up
And wiping my tears, I see Your face
You are my King, my life's an offering.

Then He twirled, holding me close
He turned around and around, in pure joy
He danced with me and took the lead.

Leaning in I danced with all my might
He held me close and there was no more night
Forgiven, loved, received, released,
He let me know I was Hand picked.

My Lord, the One, my everything
I do love You so
You picked me up and held me close
My Saviour, chosen King.
You dance with me.

Basking in His Love

I sat on a tree branch that was low to the ground
And kicked with my feet, leaves swirled all around
A carefree pose in the warm dappled shade
All serious decisions in life seemed to fade.

There I recalled Your great love for me
Your kindness and grace – that set me free
I focused on the beauty, which simmered all round
The breeze made Your presence all the more profound.

I basked in the peace and joy of your love
Knowing I could sit and in you I could trust
My future secure, life would be fine
After all, it's His now, none of it mine.

I'm basking in His love
Basking in His love
Basking in His love
In His love.

Life might bring hardship or pain
But with my hand in His, it's not in vain
Scarred from fear that once filled my heart
I can smile at the future, He's been there from the start.

Sometimes doubt and worry invade
Then His grip will tighten and again fear will fade
His presence with me, to guide and to lead
We will stand and fight, His promise true indeed.

So back on that tree branch in the real light of day
I remember my life is His to remain
Abiding in Him and dying to self
His life through mine, is a light to the world.

In times like these, I'm glad for your joy
Gives me strength to embrace each day
Staying, abiding and remaining in You
I give my life wholly to living for You.

I'm basking in His love
Basking in His love
Basking in His love
In His love.

The Rhode to Zimkesalia

28
I don't fit in — Where is home?

I've wondered many times in my life why I've felt so different. Is it because we moved house so many times? Is it because I was always the new kid on the block? Is it because I *am* different? Each of us is unique—we are uniquely and wonderfully made—I am different to those around me in lots of ways and over time I have come to accept that about myself. However, I have struggled to find where I belong, to find my fit, to find acceptance.

So this is not my HOME.

I am born to belong but I don't— I'm always uncomfortable, made for somewhere else, feeling different, not at home. Why is that?

So where is my home? Where is that place that feels secure, safe and homey? Where is the place I can be completely myself, accepted no matter what, loved, valued, free and relaxed? Where is that place called home?

Growing up in Africa and then moving to Australia, I have come to know that no place on earth is home. No matter where I am, there is still that gnawing ache for the other place that I'm currently not in. I am attached by some means— to the land, the people, the memories, the experiences, to each place I have lived—and no matter the sense of belonging and home that I experience there, it is merely a glimpse, not quite the whole.

A part of me belongs in a variety of places and so I am split, divided, my heart is in more than one place but not completely. I am torn.

For moments here in this life, we catch little glimpses of the essence of HOME. We never quite fit here on earth; we never feel utterly abandoned to the ecstasy of completeness and wholeness, of total acceptance.

I want to be honest with myself and ask myself these questions because, at the core of it all, the answer has to be that we were not designed to live in this fallen world, this place of corruption and sin. We were destined for somewhere else, a place He is preparing for us, somewhere pure and sinless—a place where we will be welcomed with open arms, cheered in through those heavenly gates, where we are loved and accepted no matter what, a place we're forgiven, heard, understood and truly loved.

Even our Saviour Jesus wasn't at home in this world. He came, suffered, was rejected, despised, mocked and not accepted. He was scarred and brutally killed and yet He came and underwent all that brutality because He was making a way for us to find our HOME. He sacrificed His comfort and acceptance and place in heaven for us to find a way home. He made it possible and then, so often, what have I done? I've rejected the very One who was doing it all for me!

Grace and thankfulness rise in me as I comprehend that His discomfort, pain and suffering happened for me; for me to find a way HOME—the place I was designed for, the place I am accepted, loved and longed for.

Home.

Give me an undivided heart that I might know Your Name God, Your Home God, Your Place God, the place I belong God, my Home in You. My Home and my heart is In You.

Kiss of Heaven

Captured by Your gaze
I'm embraced in Your grace
Your love is the Kiss of Heaven.

Stunned by Your beauty and grace
My eyes are fixed on Your face
I cannot tear myself away
Colour and light have replaced all grey
Stunned by Your beauty and grace.

Your love is the Kiss of Heaven
A love beyond compare
Your kiss declares my value
Your kiss says I'm forgiven
Your love is the Kiss of Heaven.

Standing in this place
I see love on your beautiful face
When I'm weak then You are strong
You bring freedom, joy and song
Hope has fear replaced.

Kiss me again and again
Your love is sweeter than wine.

Your love is the kiss of heaven.

Inspired by Song of Songs 1:2 (NLT)
"Kiss me and kiss me again, for your love is sweeter than wine."

29

Therefore, do not lose heart

Life is a bit like trekking through the mountains. You push up a hill and admire the wonderful view, then it's down a slippery slope and into another valley but if you keep walking you get to climb another mountain and experience the joys it brings!

When we lived in Kenya and I was sixteen years old, I got to climb Mt Kenya with a group of school friends. It was tough going. Those tracks were hard work and we were at high altitude where the weather was changeable and uncomfortable. We had a goal to walk each day to reach our camp at night and it was so far! The most we walked in a day was about eighteen kilometres and the least was thirteen—all with a heavy backpack, our clothes, bedding, food—everything we needed for the week!

When I started out, it weighed around 60lbs so it was a long hard trek each day. We were tired and hungry, suffering blisters and most of the time we were freezing cold! My girlfriend Ros and I spent a good deal of the time wondering what could possibly have possessed us to do this climb and how good it would be to have a hot bath and a hot cup of coffee once we got home.

Nevertheless, in spite of all the pain, blisters, cold and discomfort, when we reached a goal or the top of a peak and looked out over the landscape—when we could see something (sometimes the clouds were below us); when we saw the vastness of the amazing mountain wilderness we were in—we were stunned! Those mountain top experiences made us go 'wow' and we'd pause and reflect on the tiring journey to get thus far and look out in awe, aware that every step had been worth the effort and every step had given us this gift—this opportunity to witness such incredible beauty, so spectacular. I remember moments of awe that made me want to just stare and contemplate God's amazing creativity!

Each mountain top experience then gave us the motivation and fuelled us on to keep going to the next one. The memory of those mountain top experiences is what we pictured when we were struggling through melted snow—the grey slush and the darkness of the valleys, those places where we just had to keep putting one foot in front of the other and push ourselves to keep going and not give up.

And it's in those valleys that often God's rod and staff are there to comfort us. They may seem such negative, unproductive places to walk through but God is still able to work to bring to completion what He has started in us no matter whether we're on the top of a mountain or down in the deepest valley. He is never changing and always has a plan and purpose that we may not see at the time.

Another valley experience came as David and I felt God moving us out of our first home church in Australia to where, we didn't know! It took us a year of feeling unsettled and not being happy, before we took the plunge. The very first Sunday we tried our new church, we felt God saying it was right. It took us about a month to be sure but it soon became our home church.

Yes, He is faithful.

Philippians 1:6 (NIV) *"...being confident of this, that He who began a good work in you will carry it on to completion until the day of Christ Jesus."*

Romans 8:37-39 (NIV) *"No, in all these things we are more than conquerors through Him who loved us. For I am convinced that neither death nor life, neither angels nor demons, neither the present nor the future, nor any powers, neither height nor depth, nor anything else in all creation, will be able to separate us from the love of God that is in Christ Jesus our Lord."*

Isaiah 26:3,4 (NIV) *"You will keep in perfect peace those whose minds are steadfast, because they trust in You. Trust in the Lord forever, for the Lord, the Lord, is the Rock eternal."*

God has placed upon our hearts the following scripture too. Although written for Jesus, we believe it is a calling of all Christians as we grow in Christlikeness:

Isaiah 61:1-3 (NIV) *"The Spirit of the Sovereign Lord is on me, because the Lord has anointed me to preach good news to the poor. He has sent me to bind up the broken hearted, to proclaim freedom for the captives and release from darkness for the prisoners, to proclaim the year of the Lord's favour and the day of vengeance of our God, to comfort all who mourn, and provide for those who grieve in Zion – to bestow on them a crown of beauty instead of ashes, the oil of gladness instead of mourning, and a garment of praise instead of a spirit of despair. They will be called oaks of righteousness, a planting of the Lord for the display of His splendour."*

God has always reminded us to trust in Him and His sovereignty at very timely points in our walk with Him. He is so truly good, faithful and trustworthy. Praise You God. I love Your Word.

I often still miss my Mum, Jesse and Jim. I know, though, that they're with Jesus and so is our baby Leigh, the one we never knew at all. One day we will be reunited with them. I believe our absent children are growing and God gave me a picture of two little blonde haired boys running in a field with Mum and Jim and Jesus. They were so peaceful, so happy. I know too that, were Mum here, she would want us to keep living our lives fully for the Lord and testifying to His awesomeness and faithfulness so that we'll continue to do.

As we live life in our community and neighbourhood, we know that God holds our future in His hands and that we need fear no evil as He is in control. We are held fast to our anchor, our rock. Our heart's desire is that others will find hope in Jesus and know His love and power and peace as we do.

God continues to open doors for us as we are willing to walk through them. Sometimes He closes doors too. We pray that we will always be courageous, bold and obedient to His calling in spite of how impossible, painful or difficult life may seem to be.

God continues to use many sources of encouragement to build and grow us as we journey through life. Our own church and being available to be used in local ministry in whatever area He moves us into plus the impact of the Colour Conference (women's conference run by Hillsong Church, Sydney) in my life—plus many other sources and various courses we've done —have challenged and opened our eyes to live obedient to Him.

I realise now, that nothing we go through is futile!

We are on a training course, a journey, and we're learning as we go. What we go through, survive through and overcome are areas in which we will have empathy for others and in which God can use us to minister to others. We'll be serving God out of our own experiences, being there to walk alongside others, doing life and being able to offer encouragement and hope.

The seasons of life that we go through are all a part of the whole—it's the big picture, the big perspective. All seasons are required for an abundant harvest of fruitfulness. We cannot leave one season out so spring, summer, autumn and winter are all a part of God's master plan. I wonder, what season might you be in now? Take courage, as with the natural seasons of the world, this one will end and another will come and as we grow and mature, we become stronger and we can weather the seasons with less trauma.

2 Corinthians 4:16-18 (NIV) *"Therefore we do not lose heart. Though outwardly we are wasting away, yet inwardly we are being renewed day by day. For our light and momentary troubles are achieving for us an eternal glory that far outweighs them all. So we fix our eyes not on what is seen, but on what is unseen. For what is seen is temporary but what is unseen is eternal."*

As I have grown in my relationship with God, He has opened my heart to a growing compassion for people, in women's ministry, pastoral care and creativity. Part of my journey and wish for others is summed up in something I wrote one year to share with some women at an outreach dinner our church hosted:

> *As a caterpillar becomes encased in a chrysalis*
> *and is restricted as it goes through*
> *the dark place of change,*

*it slowly transforms and with much effort and struggle
pushes through a tiny opening and becomes a beautiful, strong butterfly,
ready for flight and freedom.
We all go through times of change and struggle in our lives.
We too, can change from living lives like caterpillars
to living lives in freedom like butterflies.
He (God) gave me a crown of beauty instead of ashes,
the oil of joy instead of mourning
and the garment of praise instead of a spirit of despair.
Isaiah 61:3 (NIV)
Our desire is that you know your value and potential.
You are made in the image of God.
As you become convinced and know that you are unique,
special and a 'butterfly' in the making,
we hope that you will spread your wings and fly in God's freedom!
Choose to dance, to fly, to be all you were created to be!*

There are so many worship songs with words that speak to me of hope, trust, God's faithfulness and the joy He gives us in spite of the trials we endure. I would love to write them here but I encourage you to find some beautiful worship music and allow it to minister to you. My heart in sharing this account of various aspects of my life is to offer hope and to give all the glory to God.

As we go through life, the devil wants to rob us of our peace and joy and make us feel hopeless, without a future. He wants us to view life from a defeatist, negative point of view and a position of failure. That is wrong! Don't stand for it! I won't and, even in the depths of the deepest pain, I'll choose to view it all through God's lens—His big picture perspective—and be thankful, to praise, Praise, PRAISE! TRUST in God, and keep on Praising! Live in VICTORY!

God has told me He has given me the spirit of

an overcomer. My natural wiring is negative and my humanity often displays a distorted view of life through my filter but I need the Holy Spirit on a daily, moment by moment basis—to choose to see through His filter and not my own—so that I can continue to trust Him, in spite of it all. I pray you'll know His peace and faithfulness as you put your trust in Him too.

Romans 12:2 (NIV) *"Do not conform to the pattern of this world, but be transformed by the renewing of your mind. Then you will be able to test and approve what God's will is—His good, pleasing and perfect will."*

We probably all know how powerful our thinking is. I have learned the importance of being aware of what I think, as what I think about is like a seed. It will take root and grow into something if I continue to think about it, so it's important we consider what we're thinking about and only allow good thoughts to grow, not weeds.

For far too long, I succumbed to toxic thinking. It has caused way too many problems needing to be fixed and sorted out later. As the verse above states—we are transformed by the renewing of our minds so our focus and hearts must be on what is good and right and pure and that includes trusting and keeping our hope in the midst of suffering and trials. That is why His Word is so important. We need to meditate on it day and night. It holds transformation power!

As Joni Eareckson states: *"Peace and Joy are not the absence of pain, but the Presence of God."*

And now I'll sing …

First Response

*Choose this day
Life or death
Blessing or curse
Reactive or proactive
Try it all, fail
Return, respond
No last resort
Instead first thought
No desperate plea
Instead trust
Confident
Convinced of love
Jesus, no longer last resort
Instead
Jesus, first response.*

Free to be me

Who am I?
By what am I defined?
What is my identity?
Is it what I do?
Am I way too busy?
Can I stop and be?

Yes I must,
Be, I must be.
How do I be?

Sit, listen, note
Reflect
Contemplate
Evaluate
Be, become
Accept
Peace
Be
Thank, praise
Honour
Live fully
Live real
Live thankfully
I am me
God designed
His,
Daughter
Loved
Accepted
Known
Chosen
Free to be
I am me.

The Rhode to Zimkesalia

30

Rise up and overcome!

You may very well say "But how can you just trust in God? How can you truly love a God who allows bad things to happen to you?"

I'll never forget something my Mum used to say. She said that the best place to be is in the centre of God's will. This is not to say that bad things won't happen but, if we're in the centre of God's will, what happens is then part of the bigger picture, the master plan—we'll work it through as we trust Him. His timing is perfect. Our times are in His hands. The safest, most content place to be is where God wants us. It's putting our trust in Him. Just imagine what it would be like if we didn't have Him?

Yeah, just imagine going through life, through stuff—and lots of it is really yucky stuff—without having the confidence that at least you can hang on for dear life to a Heavenly Dad who knows best and sees all things and can do and is doing what we cannot understand or fathom in our human minds. Again, we're viewing life through His lens, His filter, not our own worldly one.

When there isn't anything else to hang on to, that's when we have to hang on to God, trust Him and as in the analogy of the tapestry, have faith that He sees the upper side of 'the beautiful tapestry of life' and we only see the underside with its knots and disorganised dark threads.

Over the past few years I have suffered with some health issues which are not obvious to see but which sap me of strength and some days life is so hard, purely because everything takes so much effort. The whole of my story, in the mistakes, ill health, tragedies, all of it—is holding on to Him. He has got me through.

A few years ago, I found myself struggling so much with my health that I could barely get myself out of bed in the morning. The world was very dark and life in general was a great effort. There was a battle going on in my mind as I hung on to God, His Word and His truth. All the while my body and strength were telling me not to trust Him anymore, that He had let me down, that He no longer cared. I was depressed and sinking lower very fast.

One day I awoke and realised I was only in my mid forties and yet I felt about a hundred and ten years old. I didn't have the strength or energy to put into my kids, to support them, or love them the way they deserved to be loved. I thought about the memories I have of my Mum when I was my kids' age and realised the memories my kids would have were of me spending half my life in bed! Something had to change.

I cried out to God to help me out of this hole and determined to do whatever it took to get well again. Doctors told me there was really nothing I could do but get used to it and live with it but I know that my God is bigger than that and could bring me healing and wholeness.

So much of this battle has been in my mind. I have had to choose to make changes in spite of how I felt. I have had to listen to the Word of God and not my own doubts and fears—not the negativity that the enemy feeds me. I've had to choose to say NO! I will not listen to the lies that I am not worthy, that my best years are over, that I'm all washed up and no good to anyone anymore. I am not a failure; I am not destined to be sick until I die. I will not allow the devil to steal, kill and destroy anymore! I am designed to live life abundantly as God's word says, to live a full and flourishing life, a life where I am not merely surviving but thriving!

I had to get serious about taking every thought captive and making it obedient to God. And that required me to start counting my blessings. It was time to focus on the good things; to see what God was doing instead of what I thought He wasn't doing. I had to choose to be thankful, to be grateful for the little things—the things that seemed perhaps even trivial. But I have learned that when someone like me goes against their negative default and finds something to praise about, something to be thankful for, something to appreciate—it is powerful!

I started to count my blessings. I had two legs that were functional and two arms that worked. Yes, they might ache, but they worked. I had a supportive family. The sun was shining outside those closed curtains. I had to choose to open them and let the rays come in. I had the sense of mind to realise that I could change, that God still could use me; that He wanted to use me. I was thankful for my cups of tea—I love my tea! I was thankful for my pussycats that loved me no matter what.

When you actually start to count your blessings you will be surprised how many you can count! They add up quickly! I walked out of the front door and saw a rose in bloom. Leaning over and taking a deep breath, I inhaled the clean, fresh fragrance and felt alive! The droplet of dew tickled my nose and made me giggle! How can something so simple be so life giving and so encouraging? It was a gift from God!

God gives us blessings all the time—we just have to look and take note! I was living in a selfish world, wrapped up in my own self-absorbed pain and so blinded by self-pity that I couldn't see the beauty God was placing before me every day. For so long I had been living under a cloak of blindness, not noticing all that I had, focusing only on the physical pain I was feeling and my limitations.

So I made enquiries and the following day I signed up at a gym. I started to go for just half an hour a couple of times a week and it absolutely floored me! But I kept going and I started to walk—just 2km to start with and it would wipe me out for the day, but slowly and surely, with encouragement from my family (especially Meg who is a Personal Trainer) I began to get stronger. I saw a nutritionist who prescribed supplements for me and I started to watch what I put in my mouth a lot more carefully.

Although there were many tears and aches and pains and much temptation to give up, I knew I had to commit to this no matter the pain. I decided to set myself a goal. It was a huge goal! I registered for the Go The Extra Mile 50km fundraiser walk which, that year, was raising funds to promote the prevention of Youth Suicide. As this was something that had personally touched our family with my brother Jim, I set the goal to walk that 50km in a day. At the time I decided to do this, I was only managing a maximum of 6km at a time!

Then my husband, my daughter and my

son decided to do it as well and this was a great encouragement to me. Slowly but surely, our training regime picked up and I could feel my body getting stronger and more resilient as the weeks went by. Sometimes I would almost fall inside the house in tears—it hurt so much and I was so tired—but I persisted and with the gym workouts which were now taking about an hour, I was losing some weight, becoming toned and my whole outlook on life had changed. I had a spring in my step and I was enjoying life again!

The day of the walk arrived and with a steely determination, I started. I had friends and family praying for me and it was great—for the first half at least! Then the pain began, the rain poured down, it was cold and muddy and my mental state was struggling to cope with the enormous strain on my body.

At one point I was walking alone on a stony bush track in so much pain that my knees were ready to give up and tears poured down my face. I kept walking and just reminded myself that every step I took could save the life of someone who wanted to die and save that person's family from going through the depths of grief we had suffered over the loss of Jim. I kept going.

As I walked and prayed out loud at one point, I felt like God was picking up my feet and helping me to walk just above the ground, to relieve the pressure and pain on the inside soles of my feet that ached so much. Over 2km or so, I received three sms's from friends who were encouraging me to keep going and one of them had a picture of the angels lifting me and carrying me along the path, so my feet didn't hurt so much! I couldn't believe the similarity to the image God had shown me and I cried my thanks to Him that He was there with me, helping me through every part of the trail.

I learned something about myself that day. I learned that I am strong. I can endure. I have more inside of me that CAN do, than can't do! I realised that with God, ALL things are possible and no matter the pain and struggle along the way, if God called me to do something, He would enable me to do it! I could only see my limitations but with His help there are no limitations!

I completed the 50km walk in just over twelve hours and it was awesome to arrive at the finish line with my family cheering and congratulating me on such an achievement. Now that's much more the kind of memory I want my kids to have of me, the woman who could rise up and overcome—not the one who was a quitter and let life slip by while she slept in bed.

As mentioned before, the butterfly becomes strong and full in the wings as it has had to force itself out of a tiny hole in the cocoon. If it had it easy, its wings would just be limp and useless. The action of squeezing itself out forces the strength from the body to the wings so it can fly.

The basic fact is: God loves me. He loves you too. He IS love! His love is something we need to get a revelation of—He truly LOVES us!

Ephesians 3:14-19 (NIV) says this: *"For this reason I kneel before the Father, from whom every family in heaven and on earth derives its name. I pray that out of his glorious riches he may strengthen you with power through his Spirit in your inner being so that Christ may dwell in your hearts through faith. And I pray that you, being rooted and established in love, may have power, together with all the Lord's holy people, to grasp how wide and long and high and deep is the love of Christ, and to know this love that surpasses knowledge—that you may be filled to the measure of all the fullness of*

God."

I am so thankful for the lessons God has taught me over the years because I know I'm a better person for having learnt them (I'm still learning) and I trust I will continue to as I learn to depend on Him even more.

God has challenged me to rise up—to be the woman of God He wants me to be, to enlarge my capacity, increase my ability to fulfill His plans for me—and that is not always easy to do! It's not about me, it's all about Him and His purposes and plans and people—all of whom need to hear the love of Jesus and be saved from an eternity separated from God.

The world we live in poses challenges which oppose the Truth and the Word of God on a daily basis. My desire is to make a difference. There is much to be done.

A verse which I love and keeps me in balance is Micah 6:8 (NLT) *"O people, the Lord has told you what is good and this is what He requires of you: to do what is right, to love mercy, and to walk humbly with your God."*

In the midst of busy life, family, ministry and all the rest, we must hold true to this scripture in every way, every day, whatever we do.

A verse I love is Psalm 34:7 (NIV). It says, *"The angel of the Lord encamps all around those who fear Him, and delivers them."* Just picture that: you, in the middle of the space created when an angel stands with its large wings wrapped around you, their tips touching each other— encamped, like a tent, covered, protected, safe.

It also says '*...those who fear Him...*' that means to revere Him—I believe that is the key. Psalm 63:7 (NLT) *"Because you are my helper, I sing for joy in the shadow of your wings."*

My Prayer

"Make my life a prayer to You, dear Lord.
May I always be so true to You.
May I never be too busy, even doing good
deeds, to put You first.
Keep me balanced, may it all stay in
perspective, Your perspective.
Fill me with Your wisdom God,
May I be who You created me to be.
May I love others the way You do,
Respect and honour them
and by my actions and attitude
Show them Your love too.
Increase mercy, increase humility
Help me to grow and learn every day to be
more like Jesus.
I love you. Thank you Lord. Amen."

31

My commitment

As I have written this story of my life, I have pondered many questions, faced many painful memories and prayed through many situations, asking God to completely set me free from the chains that have bound me over the years.

— I refuse to be robbed anymore of my God-given right to live whole in Christ. I will not live broken and scarred. I have chosen to stand and be counted, to become accountable to Him, to live my life fully, to thrive, not merely survive.

— I will embrace all seasons and understand that all seasons are important for maturity and growth. I know that I need all seasons to bring an abundant harvest and that there will be fruit that has grown from being fed manure; that the crap in my life has fed the seed so that it has grown into good fruit. I understand that the pruning, which is painful at the time, also cuts off unproductive growth and encourages the good fruit to grow healthily.

— I see how important it is to be thankful. Gratitude shuts down negativity and criticism and brings breakthrough.

— My core belief is the TRUTH that is Jesus Christ my Saviour and I am anchored to Him, the rock that is higher than me.

— I choose to see God's perspective. My filter is murky.

— I choose to see myself through God's eyes. I choose to cut off the lies of the enemy and take every thought captive, making it obedient to Christ—checking it against His Word of Truth.

— I choose to believe He loves me; He will never leave me or forsake me because His Word says He won't and I believe it.

This is my story. I wonder how you felt as you read it? I pray it has given you a sense of HOPE!

I pray you have picked up some keys to help you along your way through life. I pray you'll be encouraged to allow your faith in God to grow or that you'll commit or recommit your life to God. Put your trust in Him who can do the impossible, for whom nothing is too hard, who loves you more than you can imagine.

You can do ALL things through Christ. You can!

32
Our Aussie life

Now we live in 'the land down under'—in the beautiful and rugged country of Australia, in a house on the semi-rural edge of suburbia. Life is good!

For many years, I have not felt quite as 'at home' as I do right now. Our home is lovely—we are blessed. We have space for creativity. Even our cat and dog are seemingly more at peace.

My husband is precious beyond words, I thank God for him every day, I am truly in love and so thankful. We have been married for over 30 years now. Faithful God!

Our family is precious beyond words. Our diverse and creative, gifted, musical, funny, vivacious, confident and precious kids are more of a blessing to us than words can describe. And there are just no words for our adorable grandchildren.

God is so faithful.

From humble beginnings …

Post script

It's not over yet!

God has widened our network of friendships and our sphere of influence through work, church, family and ministry. We know He works all things for our good. As we have navigated through life in Australia, we have some steadfast friendships we have made and are so grateful to God for His provision of lifelong friends.

We are keen to make an eternal difference through our connections in our community so we trust that, in all we say and do, we are a living example of Jesus and His love to all we meet. Of course, we are human and stuff up sometimes but our prayer is that the positives point to our Saviour and the negatives go unnoticed.

As we mix with people from different walks of life, we pray that our God's love for all people will shine out of us. This includes people who are hurt and those whose life experiences have left them broken. We long to see people restored and redeemed as I have been. We pray that we can become the burden bearers who help to remove people's heaviness and place it at the foot of the cross, enabling them to experience His freedom too.

We live in a very exclusive society—we're all friends when it suits but, deep down, there is an independent individuality which doesn't enable community. Jesus came for community—others. I believe in being inclusive. For so long, over many years, I have felt different, left out, excluded. Childhood experiences and the resulting damage has made me aware that I don't want to ever make people feel that way.

So I choose to be inclusive. That means to open my

home, even when it's not convenient, to be hospitable. Sometimes I prefer to be alone but it's not all about me. My life must make a difference, be like Jesus, and be a testimony to Him, which is why I write.

Having read this story, you may think you know me now. To some extent you do, but there is so much I've not written here and so much I am still learning. I know you have a story too.

It is actually quite a vulnerable feeling to put my life 'out there' but I pray my story brings insight, encouragment, hope and inspiration to you. I have also found that writing my story has helped me face issues arising from my past, bringing my hidden shame into the open and allowing God to bring healing as I've permitted Him to pinpoint those areas that were broken and needed attention.

My prayer is that this story of an ordinary girl—my story of brokenness, rebellion, sin, regret, shame, pain, fear and heartache—will be seen as a testimony of an extraordinary God, whose grace and mercy rescued me. Now I am able to stand firm and say without a doubt that My God reigns. He is my Rock, my Saviour, my Life Source, and the Lover of my soul.

In and through it all, I remind myself it's all about Him and His purpose. All glory to God. Under the shadow of His wings—He remains FAITHFUL.

The Rhode to Zimkesalia

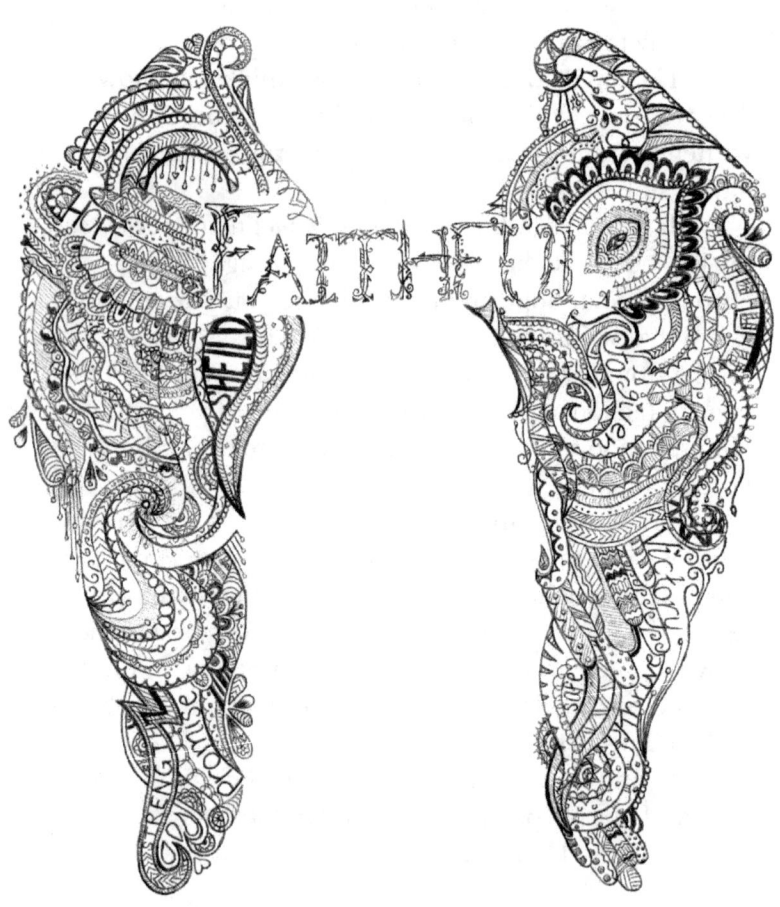

Thank You

Thanks and praises go to my Lord. Thank you for never giving up on me. Thank you for loving me; thank you for HOPE; thank you for JOY; thank you for PEACE. I love you.

So many people need to be thanked as I have embarked on this project.

To friends, counselors and professionals who have advised, edited, prayed and stuck with me on this journey of soul searching and writing. It has been quite a ride!

To those who have contributed financially to make this project come about, I am forever grateful. Your belief in me has meant so much.

Many amazing people come to mind who have been significant in my walk with God—to them, thank you.

To my Dad, I just want you to know that I am so thankful for you and I love you.

Finally and most importantly, thank you to my amazing husband, David, who has stood by me all these years and more recently helped to carry the burden of me writing. And to my children who have also walked this journey with me, I love you all.

Your response

If my story has touched you in some way and you would like to commit your life to Jesus, you might like to pray this prayer below. It is important that you mean these words from your heart:

*"Dear Lord Jesus,
I acknowledge that I am a sinner
and I am sorry for my sins and the life that I have tried to live without you;
I need Your forgiveness.
I believe that You paid the price for me,
that You died in my place for the sins I have committed,
and I am now asking You to forgive me.
You said in Your Word, Romans 10:9
that if we confess the Lord our God
and believe in our hearts that God raised Jesus from the dead,
we shall be saved.
Right now I confess Jesus as the Lord of my soul.
With my heart, I believe that God raised Jesus from the dead.
I accept you Jesus Christ as my own personal Savior
and ask You to be Lord of my life.
I give You control.
Thank You Jesus for Your unlimited grace
which has saved me from my sins.
I thank you Jesus that Your grace leads to repentance.
Therefore Lord Jesus transform my life,
restore me to wholeness
so that I may bring glory to You.
Thank You Jesus for hearing my prayer
and giving me eternal life.
Amen."*

If you would like to contact me, please feel free to do so via the details below.

Cathy Scott
cathy@zimkesalia.com.au
www.zimkesalia.com.au

*B*ibliography

Scripture quotations marked (NLT) are taken from the Holy Bible, New Living Translation, copyright ©1996, 2004, 2007, 2013 by Tyndale House Foundation. Used by permission of Tyndale House Publishers, Inc., Carol Stream, Illinois 60188. All rights reserved.

Scripture quotations marked (NIV) are taken from the Holy Bible, New International Version®, NIV®. Copyright © 1973, 1978, 1984, 2011 by Biblica, Inc.™ Used by permission of Zondervan. All rights reserved worldwide. www.zondervan.com The "NIV" and "New International Version" are trademarks registered in the United States Patent and Trademark Office by Biblica, Inc.™

Poem: Life is but a Weaving (the Tapestry Poem—unknown origin popularised by Corrie ten Boom

Because He Lives – Chorus only by Bill and Gloria Gaither © Copyright 1971 William J. Gaither, Inc. All rights controlled by Gaither Copyright Management.

Artwork: the drawings Butterfly, Angel Wings 'Faithful', Cross 'Faith', Anchor 'Hope' and Heart 'Love' © by Sarah Scott—StudioEsse.

www.ingramcontent.com/pod-product-compliance
Lightning Source LLC
Chambersburg PA
CBHW050534300426
44113CB00012B/2086